Treaty Series No. 3 (1963)

Agreement

between the Government of the
United Kingdom of Great Britain and Northern Ireland
and the Government of the French Republic

regarding the Development and Production of a Civil Supersonic Transport Aircraft

London, November 29, 1962

[The Agreement entered into force on the date of signature]

*Presented to Parliament by the Secretary of State for Foreign Affairs
by Command of Her Majesty
January 1963*

LONDON
HER MAJESTY'S STATIONERY OFFICE
EIGHTPENCE NET

Cmnd. 1916

THE BATTLE FOR CONCORDE

JOHN COSTELLO
AND TERRY HUGHES

COMPTON PRESS · SALISBURY

First published in Great Britain by
THE COMPTON PRESS LTD.
Compton Chamberlayne,
Salisbury,
Wiltshire.

8BN 900193 02 6

Designed and printed in England at The Compton Press.

This book is dedicated
to the taxpayers of Britain and France
without whom this enterprise
would not have been
possible

Acknowledgments for Illustrations

Cartoons 1 *Le Canard Enchaîné*, 2 *Lou Grant, The Los Angeles Times*, 3 *Le Canard Enchaîné*, 4 *Punch*, 5 *Guardian*, 6 *Sunday Times*, 7 *Punch*, 8 *The Los Angeles Times*, 9 *Observer*, 10 *Daily Mirror*.

Photographs: *Associated Press*, *British Aircraft Corporation*, *Pan American*, *Paul Popper Ltd.*, *Rolls Royce*, *Sud Aviation*, *Thomson Organisation*, *United Press Int.* (*UK*) *Ltd.*

Contents

Acknowledgments

CONCORDE is a highly controversial aeroplane. Whatever views people hold about the Anglo-French scheme most recognise it as one of the most important examples of contemporary technology which has been achieved across barriers of language and nationalism.

The Battle for Concorde tells the story of Concorde and how it has survived in the face of intense opposition, setting an important precedent in the politics of technology.

In assembling this account many doors have been opened by the British Aircraft Corporation and Aerospatiale whose executives, engineers and test crew have given generously of their time. Dr. A. E. Russell and Pierre Satre were especially illuminating about the origination of the project.

"Concorde is nothing, if not a political plane" and we appreciate the help given by those for whom it was a major government responsibility, especially the Rt. Hon. Anthony Wedgwood Benn, M.P., and the Rt. Hon. John Stonehouse, M.P., who were charged with the Concorde during three of its most critical years. In addition, the Rt. Hon. Duncan Sandys and Neil Marten, M.P., spared time to tell us of the early years of the project and the present Minister for Aerospace, the Rt. Hon. Frederick Corfield, helped to bring the story up to date.

Concorde concerns France as well as Britain, and we are indebted to M. Charles de Chambrun, Deputy for Lozere, and M. Jean-Jacques Servan-Schreiber, Deputy for Nancy.

The airlines have given us every assistance, in particular BOAC and Pan American.

The aircraft also has its trenchant critics and we are indebted to Dr. William Shurcliffe of Harvard, founder of the Citizens' League Against the Sonic Boom, and Richard Wiggs, founder of the Anti-Concorde project, for providing advice and much detailed information.

Mary Goldring of the *Economist* has given the authors much encouragement and informed advice.

Finally the logistics of assembling the information rivalled the complexity of Concorde itself; Mrs. Iris Hughes and Mrs. Helen Mann are by now the best informed housewives after typing the manuscript in record time. We thank them and our publisher, Julian Berry, for graciously allowing us to break more deadlines than Concorde ever could. Lastly to "Charley", who gave us more help than he ever knew.

John Costello
Terry Hughes

August 1971

— Vous avez remarqué le nez?

1

Ticket to Europe

CONCORDE was barely eleven weeks old when it met its first crisis in an elegant Paris salon. On Monday, January 14th, 1963, journalists from all over the world were summoned to a press conference at the Elysée Palace, the official residence of the President of the French Republic, General de Gaulle. As the 800-strong international press corps was checked through the wrought-iron gates by the fastidious Garde Republicaine, the newly scrubbed façades of Paris reflected the self-confidence of the Fifth Republic. Gathering beneath the glittering chandeliers, the newsmen from all over the world felt privileged to be invited to such an awesome occasion, one of President de Gaulle's rare press conferences. Stage managed with Gallic flair, it was an event which received such attention from the international press that it attracted the envy of presidents and prime ministers, both democratic and undemocratic, throughout the world. The press corps sat row upon row before a huge platform, on which stood a solitary table and chair. The television cameras were already focused, waiting for the Imperial entrance. The President's Cabinet, led by Prime Minister Georges Pompidou, took their place in the front row of the audience. Everybody knew what the subject was to be—General de Gaulle's final judgment on Great Britain's application to join the European Economic Community, the Common Market.

For over fifteen months Britain's team, led by Edward Heath, the Lord Privy Seal, had been negotiating entry terms in Brussels. Prime Minister Harold Macmillan was determined to lead Britain in the direction of Europe, despite the hostility of some of his own supporters who sought an independent role for Britain in world affairs. But Macmillan, who had come to power in the wake of the Suez disaster, knew that there could be no post-Imperial glory, Britain had neither the strength nor resolve to stand alone as a world power. Her ailing economy and industries demanded membership of a wider group—the Common Market. Particularly important were the needs of the technological industries—electronics, computers, atomic energy and aerospace, where access to a large market was important, not only in making these industries more competitive, but also in creating bigger investment resources necessary to fund research and development. At the beginning of the 1960s it was apparent to France and Britain that their technological industries could not stand alone against world competition, particularly from the United States.

In a historic broadcast on September 21st, 1962, Harold Macmillan told the British nation that it was "no good pretending that we can go back to the old world before the war". He spelt out his reasons for Britain joining Europe, and at the heart of them was a plea for British technology, a dowry he knew he could offer Europe. "Britain", he said "should make not just the things which anybody can learn to make, but the difficult things which need precision and highly skilled workmanship". He catalogued the special skills which Britain possessed—"nuclear stations, computers, supersonic aircraft". Much of what he said in his reassuring Edwardian style about Britain's desire to enter the Community sounded like a proposed merger between two well-established, but successful corporations.

"Well, it's been a great success up to now. They form a great economic group. . . . And so you see Western Europe is quite different from the Commonwealth. They are both going concerns, but different."

Towards the end of his script, the Prime Minister who, as Lieutenant Macmillan, had witnessed the slaughter on the Western Front in the First World War, allowed a personal note to enter. "Many of us," he paused for a moment, "especially those who are young in heart or in years, are impatient of the old disputes, intolerant of the obsolete conceptions; anxious that our country should take its part and if possible a leading part, in all these new and hopeful areas." Here was a clear plea to Gaullist France as much as to a bright new British technology, which could not grow sturdily in a walled English garden.

Despite Macmillan's eloquent pleas, everyone sitting at the Elysée Conference on the afternoon of January 14th, 1963, knew that the key to Europe was in de Gaulle's hand. The General disliked the Common Market with its grey bureaucrats arguing endlessly over the price of olive oil. For him history demanded a more glorious style of leadership. According to Macmillan, his was a Napoleonic view of Europe.

"He lived in the past. He lived in the world where he thought a single country of Europe could dominate."

De Gaulle believed that France should lead Europe to a new position of power and influence against the Superpowers, especially the United States. If Europe did not reassert herself she would be "Atlanticised". The rekindling of Europe's technology was essential to de Gaulle's scheme. It was clearly beyond the power of one European nation, even France, to withstand American and eventually Japanese and Russian competition. Britain, with her strong technological industries, spending more on scientific research and development than any other European country, could play a part in this grand scheme to regenerate a Continent. Whatever the General's lofty thoughts implied, Britain herself believed that her survival depended on a robust technology. Prestige was not enough, scientific inventiveness had to compensate for lack of resources.

National prestige in the middle of the twentieth century was no longer a matter of armies and dreadnoughts, but depended on computers, atom-smashers and jet airliners. Scientific prowess had in some way replaced the older military glories. Russia had launched her first Sputnik in 1957, and had raced ahead with a manned space flight programme. The United States, having got off to a disastrous start in the space race—Khrushchev had contemptuously dismissed her first space satellite as a "grapefruit"—was now chasing Russia hard. Both de Gaulle and Macmillan had been at the summit of politics in two of the world's most nationalistic countries long enough to understand instinctively the value of prestige projects. It was perhaps ironic that the decisions on such complex and far-ranging matters in a changing Europe should lie with two leaders who seemed so much a part of a vanished world. In Cabinet Macmillan had reportedly spoken of his great aunt's Daimler, which had travelled at the "sensible speed" of thirty miles an hour. The great advantage of that particular vehicle, as the Prime Minister wistfully reminded his colleagues, was that one could enter it without removing one's top hat. But though his manner might be that of an Edwardian proconsul, Harold Macmillan noted that many people liked to travel at greater speeds, and enjoying the allusion pressed his colleagues into agreeing that Britain ought to cater for this profitable modern eccentricity by building a supersonic airliner. De Gaulle on his side of the Channel spoke of *la gloire* and "cried that France should lead the world, almost living in the state of Louis XIV".

Criticising the decision to start Concorde Anthony Wedgwood Benn, former Minister of Technology, said of the early sixties, "European technological co-operation meant finding something very big and dramatic and exciting, which was within your capability and doing it."

The Anglo-French Concorde was exactly such a project.

On both sides of the Channel, the French and British aircraft industries had been working on an airliner which would fly faster than sound. Each had come to the conclusion that the only way to challenge the Americans, who possessed over 85% of the world civil aviation market, was to make a technological leap ahead. The aircraft engineers had reasoned that since high speed air travel was inevitable, then the first successful supersonic transport would scoop the market.

The British aircraft companies thought speed was highly marketable. They believed man would always take the fastest route—and pay for it. Sir George Edwards, at that time Managing Director of Vickers Armstrong, suggested in his Presidential lecture to the Royal Aeronautical Society in 1958 that,

"There is a definite connection between industry, population and speed of transport."

In his view Britain's industrial development may have been heavily influenced by this factor. Certainly any study of the growth of travel and commerce showed speed to be an important consideration.

The American companies were very strong competitors, backed by first rate engineering, efficient production and a large home market. The Federal government stood behind them, financing research and development with military contracts. Yet the European industries had proved themselves capable of building aircraft years ahead of their U.S. rivals in the civil aviation market. Britain had flown the world's first commercial jet transport in 1949, the ill-fated Comet 1, which had appeared five years ahead of the Boeing 707. Sud-Aviation of France had produced the first medium-range pure jet airliner, the Caravelle in 1956, with almost as great a lead over its American rivals. The Caravelle made France's name in civil aviation, selling even in the highly competitive American home market. Despite this technological brilliance, however, the hard fact remained that America dominated world aviation with only a few traditional outlets left for British and French aircraft; and American companies not only built excellent products, they also made money out of them. It was significant to the British and French aircraft constructors that the commercial successes they had experienced had also been technical breakthroughs. The British had made money out of the Viscount, the world's first turbo-prop short haul airliner, and the French Caravelle had been profitable. Therefore, in the view of Pierre Satre, Chief Designer of Aerospatiale, responsible for the Caravelle and later the Concorde, "If we build an aircraft very similar to an existing one there are no possible sales." Europe had to make a technological leap to survive.

Certainly in the late fifties the British industry was in need of success. Its future was uncertain. The traditional military markets were diminishing. Macmillan had ordered a study of Britain's defences after taking office in 1956, and Duncan Sandys, Minister of Defence, produced a White Paper. Among its proposals Section 61 declared, "The Government has decided not to go ahead with the development of a supersonic manned bomber which could not be brought into service in much under ten years." Another recommendation proposed that there should be no further work on fighters after the P1 (Lightning), laconically adding for the attention of the aviation firms that a "certain amount of disturbance is unavoidable." Britain was to rely on missiles. These, however, were equally short-lived—the £100 million Blue Streak programme had to be scrapped in 1961 because of its obsolescence. Whatever the military consequences, it was clear that the future of the aircraft industry would have to lie in civil projects. Government aeronautical and research establishments stepped up research on commercial aviation projects. A Supersonic Transport Aircraft Committee (STAC) was formed in 1956 and millions were spent at the Royal Aircraft Establishment at Farnborough and other centres researching into supersonic airliners. This paid off handsomely. By 1959 Britain was further ahead than any other country in the world, and felt confident that as a result of a number of breakthroughs commercial supersonic aircraft were practical. Moreover, they felt confident, and advised the Government accordingly that now was the time to build a plane and put British aviation on top again.

Britain had been in this position before, but the price for being first, and failing, had been high. The Comet 1, which came into service with BOAC in 1952, met disastrous problems of metal fatigue. After five years of redesigning, it emerged as the Comet IV, by then too small and too late to compete with the larger Boeing 707. The lessons of being out in front have never been forgotten by the British aviation industry—nor has the prestige. The British aircraft industry badly needed another world beater like the Vickers Viscount to restore its sense of confidence. The British companies also knew that their industry was too fragmented and badly organised to take on a major world-beating project. Mergers were in the air.

The Report of the Farnborough Committee, recommending that Britain should go supersonic, looked like a gleam of light in a dark dawn. There were, however, major snags. To capture the world market, the Americans would have to be beaten to the post; the Comet had shown this to be a risky business. Also any supersonic aircraft was likely to cost a great deal of money—far more than Britain could afford alone. There were signs that British opinion was losing patience with the bright, but expensive, ideas of the aviation industry. An editorial in the London *Times* of February 16th, 1960, said,

"Current work makes at first sight an impressive show, and if the list is drawn up—the V.C.10, V.C.11, the PH 121, the Rotodyne, the Vanguard, the Argosy, the Herald, and so on (not to mention one or two new service aircraft)—everything may look set fair. But there is too much research on hand—into vertical take off, supersonic flight, high lift and other matters, . . . it is hard to escape the impression of a lack of direction and decision."

Decisions would have to be taken quickly if Britain was to be in the next generation of civil jet transports. But the Government wondered where the money was coming from. An obvious answer was to try America. A mission was dispatched across the Atlantic, but the American industry was doing very nicely out of the current boom in subsonic jets, which had entered airline service in 1957, and was opposed to an early introduction of supersonics. Moreover, they hinted at plans to build a bigger, faster and more technically advanced aircraft than Britain. The French seemed the logical partners, even before the Common Market negotiations opened. Their industry was much smaller than the British, but they had made a comeback in world aviation with aircraft like the Mystère, Mirage and Caravelle and they had supersonic plans.

The Caravelle had been built by Sud-Aviation, whose boss, Georges Héreil, was one of the most dynamic men in French industry, and unlikely ever to undervalue the work of Sud-Aviation. He had arrived at Sud-Aviation when it was on the financial rocks, with the task of clearing up the company's finances, if necessary by liquidation. Instead of being forced out of business, Héreil started the Caravelle in 1951 and made Sud's fortune. The successful design team, led by Pierre Satre and Lucien Servanty, wanted to make another technological leap with a supersonic successor to the Caravelle, the Super-Caravelle.* Approaches were made to the French by British aircraft companies. An attraction of co-operation with France was the captive airline—Air France, and the traditional French markets in Europe and Africa. But were the interests of Britain and France the same? Both of them had the ability to build an SST†, both needed to share the cost, but both wanted a foothold in the American market, and at the outset would have preferred an American partner, rather than a European one. The Americans, however, were not interested, they were unconvinced of the commercial value of an SST programme at that stage. Perhaps a leading Gaullist Deputy was right when he said "The French are very capable people, very good at dreaming up things, but they have no sense of commerce. Concorde is the first time that the English have joined them in this."

The French might seem the logical partners for Britain—they were also the last chance, and the chance was not missed. They were sceptical, however, when invited to Farnborough to see the work of the STAC group, but were hopefully interested. On the highest instructions Whitehall dispatched a copy of the top secret STAC report to France in 1959. When the Bristol engineers found out, they were exasperated, "Some clot at the Aviation Ministry, one of the Admin. boys, gave the report to France." The leak had the desired effect; a year later not only were the French aeronautical engineers as convinced about the project as their British counterparts, but under the presiding genius, Georges Héreil, designs were actually being produced and wind tunnel testing was well under way for a Super-Caravelle.

Britain did not stand still. Preliminary design studies were commissioned by the Ministry of Aviation, and in the space of a few months after the 1959 Election the aircraft industry was dramatically reorganised. Duncan Sandys, who, as Defence Minister, had been responsible for the defence re-shaping of 1957, was given this exacting task. He remembered that,

"After the Election, about November, I got the aircraft manufacturers together, there were about fifteen of them. I said 'I think there is only room for two.' They agreed there ought to be amalgamations of some sort and felt that it would take no doubt a number of years to achieve it. I said 'Let's see whether we can do it by Christmas'.

* The French proposal for a supersonic Super-Caravelle in the early 1960s should not be confused with the subsonic Super-Caravelle at present flying on the world's air-routes.

† SST is an abbreviation for Supersonic Transport.

So what I did was to set up a 'marriage bureau' in my office. Every week I suggested that firms come and see me and I would propose 'marriages', and they would tell me how they got on. It went very well. We didn't achieve it by Christmas, but we did achieve it by Twelfth Night."

The two groups which emerged were the British Aircraft Corporation and Hawker Siddeley. Bristol Aircraft, which had done a great deal of work on the SST, joined BAC. Both groups were asked to present fuller designs for an SST. After careful study by the Ministry of Aviation, BAC were chosen to continue the work and were asked to produce a draft design by August 1961. But the French sprang a surprise at the Paris Airshow, by unveiling Sud-Aviation's model of a medium range Super-Caravelle. On French television Georges Héreil confidently predicted that it would come into service in 1967, taking Sud-Aviation and France into world leadership.

The construction of the French supersonic plane, recalled one of his advisers, was to be seen as General de Gaulle's "Technical Austerlitz". But Héreil's plan to steal a march on the British had one weak point—the engine. On any aeroplane the engines are an important factor, for the supersonic plane they would be absolutely crucial, and France had no suitable engines to power her Super-Caravelle. When the chips were down, their drive for the technological leadership of Europe was going to depend on buying an American or British engine. The Anglo-Saxons were indispensable, after all. To develop a suitable power unit would have cost more than the airframe, and with France's limited experience would have taken many years, sacrificing the vital lead over the United States. As it happened the British had been developing a supersonic engine, the Olympus for the TSR2, and millions of pounds had already been spent in proving it. It was a bonus ace that the British knew they could play at the right time.

The Governments moved towards a deal. Duncan Sandys, the British Minister of Aviation, had already agreed with Robert Buron, his French opposite number, that there was no objection to the collaboration of British and French firms on private ventures. This could include an SST. In early 1960 Sandys visited the major French companies—Sud-Aviation, Dassault and Nord. The funds required would be on a far larger scale than the private aircraft companies could provide in France and Britain and it was inevitable that the research and development would be financed by the two Governments. The French were anxious about the cost, but Sandys had swung the British Cabinet with little resistance,

"I remember saying to the Cabinet—'If we're not in the big

supersonic aircraft business, then it's really just a matter of time before the whole British aircraft industry packs up. It's obviously the thing of the future. It may pay. It may not pay. We can't afford to be out of it.' "

If the French government, conscious of costs, wanted to find a partner, the French company was not, at first, receptive to the idea of a joint project. As far as Georges Héreil's team were concerned they believed they knew the answers, and there was no question of surrendering design leadership. What they wanted, at the most, was to share engine development, parts of the airframe and production technique. Britain, however, wanted somebody to share the cost of her own SST and knew that the French needed British engines. High level diplomatic exchanges between Whitehall and Paris began to work for a change in attitude. As the team at Sud progressed with the elementary design work, in spite of initial confidence they realised that the inevitable problems of supersonic flight were not going to be easy to solve. It was left to the Ministers to suggest that BAC and Sud should produce a common design. But the two proposals submitted by the French and British companies in November 1961 were far from being common. Sud produced plans for a medium range supersonic whilst BAC submitted a long range design which differed in many details. Sud wanted to get it into production fast, believing that they could persuade the Americans to keep to the long range market, still believing that the example of the Caravelle could be followed. This was good Gallic logic but did not suit the British. The main French routes radiated out from Paris to all parts of Europe, the Mediterranean, North Africa, and beyond. The North Atlantic and long-haul routes to Australia and the Far East were particularly important to the British. Georges Héreil openly tried to interest the Americans in keeping to the long range market when giving the Spellman lecture in Delft in 1961. It was greeted with indifference. According to Pierre Satre,

"The people interested in Boeing, Lockheed and Douglas, they were well aware of this proposal. But the American people at that time thought probably that the American industry would cover the complete field."

The British, from bitter experience with the Comet IV, realised that only a long range plane would sell, and an aircraft which could not cross the North Atlantic was a non-starter. In the British, and eventually French view, although the combined markets of Air France and BOAC were good starting points for world sales, it would have to be eyeball-to-eyeball competition with the United States.

The negotiations to enter the Common Market had now been

opened in earnest and it was already becoming clear that Britain had to gain French co-operation and acceptance, but the engineers were still a long way apart, and Macmillan's Government wanted a dramatic gesture to Europe as quickly as possible.

In late December, the new Minister of Aviation, Peter Thorneycroft, was dispatched to Paris to meet the Minister of Transport, Robert Buron; the result was a request to both companies to "co-operate in formulating a joint outline project" which the Ministers pointedly expected to receive early in 1962. But the diplomacy of the aero-engineers was becoming intolerably slow, there were substantial differences of approach and Managing Director of BAC, Sir George Edwards "sometimes doubted whether we would ever see it through together". Underlying the attempts to produce a design, he felt there was a basic mistrust. "Albion is still likely to be perfidious in French eyes." The design plans did not appear. To disguise the lack of progress a statement was issued saying that the "two companies had arrived at a preliminary design" and were "to be invited jointly to undertake a design study and other preparatory work to enable the governments to reach a decision". July was the deadline but by the autumn they had still to appear.

Time was running out, and the constant persuasion, checking and alteration that slowly brought the two concepts together, dragged on and were not ready by the 1962 Farnborough Air Show, where it had been planned to announce the final designs.

Waiting for the aircraft companies to get together was beginning to tax everybody's patience. The British government found a temporary substitute for the long awaited SST agreement by offering the abandoned £100 million Blue Streak rocket to the European Space Research Organisation to be developed by ELDO (European Launcher Development Organisation), saving several thousand jobs at Hawker Siddeley. The British and French designers finally reached agreement in an unconventional way. Tired of all the endless meetings, Lucien Servanty, the senior Sud-Aviation designer, called at the Paris hotel of Dr. Strang, BAC's chief designer, and took him to a small factory in a remote Paris suburb, where nobody could find them. They locked themselves in and working hour after hour through a haze of *Gitanes*, they sketched out the first Concorde. To the Englishman it was a new style.

"It's very unusual to do it in this fashion. It's very much the sort of thing you think of as a schoolboy. It very rarely happens in real life."

At the beginning of October 1962, the long awaited document arrived at the Ministry of Aviation. It was just twenty pages long.

In aviation terms "little more than a sketch", but to the politicians on both sides of the Channel, it was the blueprint for political objectives. Without actually digging the Channel Tunnel under the Straits of Dover, there was no better way of linking the two countries. France could now go ahead to build a bigger aircraft industry with British support, and Britain could secure acceptance in Europe with French goodwill. No time was lost in preparing the treaty which was seen as a passport to Europe and an enormous boost to Britain's Common Market hopes. In any event, as one Cabinet Minister put it,

"I would say that what we did with the Anglo-French Concorde was create a little Common Market of our own, for that one project!"

If Britain had a little Common Market with the General, most people thought it must inevitably lead to a bigger Common Market with the rest of Europe, and government sources confidently predicted that the next treaty to be signed would be the Treaty of Rome itself. The Anglo-French Supersonic Aircraft Agreement was completed on November 29th, 1962, at Lancaster House in London, by Julian Amery, the new Minister of Aviation, himself a francophile, and the French Ambassador Geoffroy de Courcel, a close confidant of the General in 1940 and known appropriately as the "First Gaullist". The Agreement reflected the still unresolved argument about what kind of supersonic aircraft it would be and some of the leading French engineers even thought they would have to build two, especially as the Agreement called for both a medium and a long range version to be built, with Article 6 requiring that "Every effort shall be made to ensure that the programme is carried out both for airframe and engine, with equal attention to the medium and long range versions". Article 1 also made it quite clear that "The principle of this collaboration shall be the equal sharing of the work and of the expenditure incurred by the two Governments and of the proceeds of sales." The really far-reaching nature of the Agreement was shown in Article 4 which stipulated that "integrated organisations of the airframe and engine firms shall be set up." This was a revolutionary proposal with far-reaching consequences, not just for aviation, but applicable to a whole range of advanced industries. It was to be industrial re-organisation on a continental scale.

Next step Europe. On the same day that Julian Amery signed the Agreement and explained its purpose to the London press, the British Ambassador in Washington was holding a press conference to tell the Americans that Britain was confident of joining the Common Market as one of its leading members before the end of

1963. In London the Aviation Minister assured a sceptical press that "steps have been taken to control the costs" on a project in which Britain's share would be £75-85 million, spread over eight years. It looked like a bargain, especially when compared to the £100 million spent on Blue Streak, and the soaring price of TSR2. The future for the plane and Britain's aircraft industry looked bright, it appeared to have "every chance of securing a substantial part of the world market", but *The Times* was less enthusiastic. Under a leader entitled SUPERSONIC GAMBLE it discerned a "venture bristling with risks", the biggest being that of losing the lead to America. But London's most influential paper took the message about Europe; it saw this as an "important experiment in European co-operation" with hints at further projects ahead.

The Anglo-French Agreement had been signed and Macmillan's government was convinced that it had a ticket to Europe. Only the details remained to be cleared up, and the plane actually built. If the Agreement showed Britain's willingness to integrate one of her key industries with Europe, it was for de Gaulle to decide whether Britain was suitable for entry to the Common Market. The General thought he knew his Anglo-Saxons. Every argument used by the British government to convince the electorate showed that they expected to reassert British influence in the world through the Common Market, challenging France for the leadership. It was to be a substitute for Empire. Another agreement made with another President that year seemed far more significant to de Gaulle. The Nassau Agreement, made with President Kennedy in December 1963 following the Cuban missile crisis, reaffirmed Britain's special relationship with the United States. How could de Gaulle prevent Europe being "Atlanticised" if Britain was to be the "Trojan horse" as the Gaullist press called her.

The time of decision had arrived; Britain's ticket was on the table that morning in the Elysée Palace. A reverent calm fell over the journalists as the tall figure of the General appeared from behind the velvet curtains to deliver his verdict. The climax of years of diplomatic activity, months of negotiations in Brussels, Paris and London had arrived. The General knew his words would make history, and he did not disappoint his audience. Speaking without notes, calm and relaxed, he began to expound his thoughts with magisterial emphasis. England, it seemed, had asked to enter the Common Market on her own terms, and this had posed "problems of a very great dimension". She could not yet bring herself to accept the European Community "without restriction, without reserve".

This was the conclusion that the General had drawn from the

"long, so long, so long" (with carefully deliberate emphasis) Brussels negotiations. This was what Macmillan feared; France was diplomatically closing the door in Britain's face. But the General was astute enough to know that even if he kept Britain out this time, he still had to allow for possible future entry and good working relationships with her. The Concorde was a part of de Gaulle's plan. Britain had to be held to the Agreement. As an alternative to immediate entry, "if the Brussels negotiations were not to succeed" he held out the alternative of "an accord of association". "Nothing," he deliberately emphasised, "would prevent close relationship and direct co-operation as the two countries have proved by deciding to build together the supersonic aircraft Concorde". At a stroke he had outmanoeuvred any plan Macmillan might have considered for withdrawal from the project, for the President made it clear that if "Britain's own evolution and the evolution of the universe" was to bring the English "little by little" towards the Continent and "one day, perhaps, will lead it to moor alongside" then part of the evolutionary process would be judged on British performance on the Concorde. At the same time as his words brought the Concorde's *raison d'être* dangerously close to collapse, the General christened the project officially, to the amazement of the French officials. The name "Concord" had first been suggested by the ten-year-old son of a BAC official. The name had been passed up through the echelons of BAC and the Ministry of Aviation to be greeted with approval by the Minister, Julian Amery. When passed to France the suggestion was greeted with disdain—"too static" they said, it sounded like a well known square in Paris and was spelt with an extra letter in the French language. On January 13th, 1963, de Gaulle ignored his officials. It was, perhaps, a subtle concession to wounded English pride.

Had this press conference taken place ten weeks earlier, there is little doubt the Concorde project would have been stillborn. Had de Gaulle slammed the door before the completion of the Anglo-French Supersonic Agreement the indications are that the Ministry of Aviation and the Treasury would have demanded a more detailed design and cost analysis. If the European pressure had not been so great the British Cabinet might have been dissuaded from supporting an open-ended commitment to what was little more than a sketch.

In the judgment of one former Minister, "If it is true that it was insisted on by Macmillan to get us into Europe, it was certainly the most expensive, non-effective ticket of entry to anything."

LOU GRANT—THE LOS ANGELES TIMES

"SST"

2

The Great Paper Plane Race

THE DECISION to proceed with Concorde was a bold one. As design teams settled down in Filton and Toulouse, to tackle the problems of supersonic flight, the world's airlines were buying American aircraft as fast as they rolled off the assembly lines. British aircraft held only a small percentage of the world market. There had been many brilliant prototypes, but few commercial successes. The French had sold the Caravelle to United Airlines, breaking into the American market for the first time, but the British, experienced in selling in the big league, knew the French were over-optimistic. "They were drunk on selling twenty Caravelles", was the uncharitable but accurate comment of BAC.

The financial and technological risks of the Anglo-French decision were enormous. In 1960, the Minister of Aviation told the Cabinet squarely that "if we miss this generation, we will never catch up again. We'll end up making executive aircraft." The construction of an SST would stretch the planemaker's ability to the very frontiers of known aviation technology. The conditions of supersonic flight were not entirely unknown, military pilots had broken the sound barrier many times since the end of the war, but there were vast areas of ignorance, particularly in the matter of flying large, faster-than-sound aircraft. Much of the experience was American. On October 14th, 1947, Captain Charles Elwood Yeager climbed into the Bell X-1 rocket plane at Edwards Air Force Base, California, and, 70,000 feet over the Nevada desert, opened up the throttle. As the plane accelerated towards Mach 1,* the speed of sound, it was increasingly buffeted by shock waves and turbulence but once through the "sound barrier", the flight became smooth again. On a series of forty-one brief sorties, some approaching twice the speed of sound, the Bell X-1 provided a mass of scientific information. It

* A Mach number is the accepted way of relating an aircraft's velocity to the speed of sound which is not constant but which varies according to the temperature of the atmosphere. Named after Ernest Mach, an Austrian physicist, Mach 1 is normally 760 miles an hour at sea level. Concorde's design speed of Mach 2.2 is about 1,430 miles an hour at 60,000 feet.

proved that controlled flight was possible beyond the sound barrier. Five years after the flight of Bell X-1, squadrons of supersonic fighters were becoming operational in the American forces.

The difference between high performance fighters and supersonic transports, whether bombers or airliners, is very great. The problems of flying supersonic, even relatively small fighters like the F.100 and Mig 21, had been tackled on vast defence budgets in the West and Russia, and their solution owed much, in the words of a leading aircraft engineer, to "brute force and bloody ignorance", or as one distinguished American designer put it—"give me an engine big enough and I'll give you an ironing board that'll fly supersonic".

Supersonic fighters are basically light airframes built round colossal engines. They do not have to carry more than two passengers or cross the Atlantic non-stop; and defence chiefs are more concerned with the ability to shoot down enemy planes on brief intercepting missions, than with fuel economy or cost efficiency. To build a supersonic bomber is a much greater problem, it needs a long range and large pay-load; its requirements are very similar to those of a supersonic airliner.

The research undertaken by the STAC at the Royal Aircraft Establishment, Farnborough had evolved a number of theoretical solutions to the problems of flying large aircraft supersonically, but many answers could only be ascertained in the conditions of real flight. A prototype would be needed. All the years of study, however, had shown that a successful supersonic transport depended on two major factors. First, an aerodynamic shape had to be created which could be flown at both subsonic and supersonic speeds. For subsonic flight, aircraft need large straight wings, to provide stable lift, but as an aircraft approaches the speed of sound the most suitable configuration is a narrow swept-back wing. Since any supersonic plane has to take off and land at low speeds, there is a basic design conflict. The second problem is the "heat barrier". At very high speeds the friction of air particles rushing past the aircraft's surface causes the skin temperature to rise. At twice the speed of sound it reaches the boiling point of water which is approaching the temperature at which the aluminium alloys traditionally used for aircraft construction lose their strength.

When the STAC team got to work, all the research undertaken on supersonic aircraft had been based on the theory that airflow clings to the wing, both on its upper and lower surfaces; lift is provided because pressure on the concave underside of the wing is greater than the pressure on the convex topside. This is the classical theory of aerodynamics. But when a plane goes faster than sound, the undisturbed air particles in front of the leading edge of the wing instead of parting smoothly, receive no advance warning of its approach, so that a supersonic plane punches its way through the atmosphere, creating turbulence and resistance. It can be compared to the difference between walking through water slowly and the resistance met when trying to run. The swept-back wing has been evolved to cope with this problem. The nose of an aircraft spreads a V-shaped shock wave behind it, like a ship's bow-wave. This is called a Mach Cone; its angle depending on the speed at which the plane is travelling. The wings are swept back to keep them inside the Mach Cone, so that the stable airflow inside the cone provides lift, passing smoothly over the wing surfaces. This is vital, because should this airflow become disturbed it ceases to be attached to the wings, lift becomes erratic and the plane becomes uncontrollable. Sweepback is used in this way to "cheat the Mach number" but at a price; because aircraft with high sweepback do not perform well at low speeds they have to land fast "like bats out of hell".

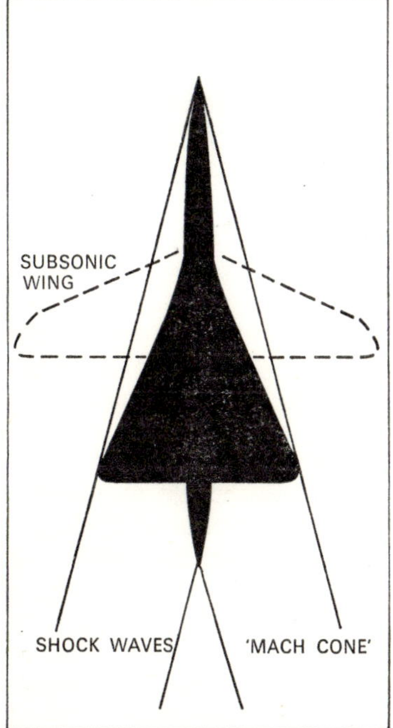

CHEATING THE MACH NUMBER
Straight subsonic wings are swept back inside the mach cone to give stable lift at supersonic speeds.

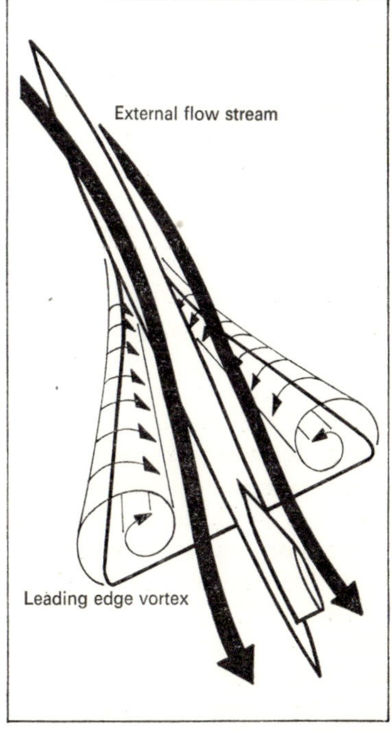

THE GIANT PAPER DART
Airflow curling over the delta edge forms a vortex to give added lift and stability at all speeds.

This is all very well for a fighter pilot but the performance is hardly likely to appeal to nervous airline passengers.

That a civil supersonic aircraft could be built at all was due to the pioneer work carried out at Farnborough in the mid-fifties by a German engineer, Dr. Dietrich Kuchemann. He was one of Farnborough's post-war "recruits", from the high-powered Luftwaffe teams who had worked on the Reich's jet fighters. Kuchemann's analysis started from the simple aerodynamic shape, the paper dart. One reason why the paper dart flies so well, he realised, is the sharp leading edge, which instead of creating a smooth airflow over the wings, also produces a detached airflow which gives the dart most of its lift. This flow takes the form of vortices, rolls of air curling over the sharp leading edges; the net result is a substantial contribution to lift and stability at all speeds. At transonic and supersonic speeds this detached vortex airflow is so strong that it cannot be disturbed by influences which might upset a wing dependent entirely upon attached airflow.

In the summer of 1956 it looked as though Kuchemann's detached airflow produced with a narrow delta wing would give the necessary lift/drag ratio to make supersonic flight a commercial reality. It was this work which persuaded the British Government to support the project with the STAC, which drew its members from the ablest men in Britain's aircraft firms, government research departments and airlines.

The Committee probed all areas of supersonic flight, from suitable designs to operational routes. A major problem emerged immediately. At the beginning of the research, it looked as though the paper dart, whatever its advantages at supersonic speed, would mean relatively low lift at low speed, resulting in extremely fast landings, with the nose having to be tilted well up. In the United States, research had been conducted into narrow delta wings for over ten years, and the view was that they became uncontrollable if hit by sideways gusts of wind on landing. This was thought to occur at angles of incidence greater than three degrees; but to land at three degrees or less would mean touching down at over 500 m.p.h. and even "bats out of hell" could hardly do this. If delta planes were to be landed at anything approaching normal speeds, their angle of incidence would need to be over thirteen degrees. In spite of Kuchemann's breakthrough with the paper dart, it looked as though the delta wing would have to be abandoned in favour of conventional swept wings.

If American research were accepted, then Kuchemann's approach to supersonic civil flight was impossible. One man at Farnborough, an ex-World War I fighter pilot, refused to accept the American conclusions. He began his own experiments with a step ladder, a Heath Robinson model launcher and a camera. After a brilliantly simple series of tests, W. E. Gray was able to prove the Americans wrong. The critical angle for the narrow delta was shown to be well over fifteen degrees, and depended on the ratio of the length to the width of the delta. Wind tunnel tests confirmed his basic theory, and later flights with the HP115 research aircraft showed the delta was in fact stable to an angle of thirty degrees. In March 1959, the STAC was able to offer such encouraging figures on lift/drag ratio for the slender delta, that preliminary design studies were set in motion. The dangers of delay were becoming all too apparent.

In the United States the Pentagon had been commissioning research into supersonic flight for defence purposes. Despite the growing importance of missiles, the United States Air Force still believed in the potency and flexibility of the strategic bomber. If a supersonic manned bomber were built for the American defence programme, a supersonic airliner would be only a short step away. This had been the classic route to success of Boeing's highly profitable 707, developed from the KC 135 air tanker.

In the early 1950s General Curtis LeMay, Commander of the United States Strategic Air Force, had begun looking for a supersonic bomber. After four years' work, Bomber LeMay wanted to see the designs. He was not impressed. They had relied on the "brute force" concept and projected a 500-ton monster whose enormous engines needed so much fuel that each plane would have to carry two jettisonable fuel tanks, each as big as a B-47. The General, known for his plain speaking, took one look, almost swallowed his cigar, and bellowed: "this isn't an aeroplane, it's a three ship formation". It was a nose-dive into the waste-paper basket.

Three years later the designers came up with the B-70 bomber, an incredible "futuristic" aircraft made of stainless steel and titanium. Designed to fly at three times the speed of sound its sinister shape justified the name "Valkyrie". It was to be built by North American, which had built one of America's first supersonic fighters. The SST lobby, centred on the Federal Aviation Agency, saw their chance. General Elwood Quesada, first Administrator of the FAA, certainly believed that the B-70 could become a prototype for a Mach 3 American SST to keep the U.S. ahead in the commercial market. Compared to such an aircraft, the Concorde would be both smaller and slower. In 1959 he drew President Eisenhower's attention to British and French schemes to scoop the U.S. in flying the first civil supersonic. "Ever since the Wright Brothers' memorable accomplishment in 1903," argued Quesada in a FAA report, "the military establishment has had a vigorous development programme."

The report continued "For over fifty years commercial aviation has had the advantage of leaning on and borrowing from a strong military development programme." The President was not receptive; his advisers had told him that the manned bomber, supersonic or not, had no future, and so billions of dollars could be saved on its development. The B-70's days were numbered. Militarily it had attracted the fatal Pentagon tag of "the paper airplane which would fly in a cardboard sky"; the U.S. Chiefs of Staff were engrossed in the missile race with Russia.

On November 30th, 1959, the fateful telex clattered through to the headquarters of North American Aviation, the B70's builders, "CEASE ALL STUDY DESIGN DEVELOPMENT AND FABRICATION AND TEST WORK TOWARDS B70 WEAPON SYSTEM". With this message the Pentagon defaulted on its traditional role as patron of United States' civil transport aircraft. An influential Senator, Lyndon B. Johnson, protested. In his view the cancellation threatened long term American superiority in commercial aviation. If the B70 development were stopped, then effective research into a civil supersonic transport would stop. "Transportation of people and cargo at three times the speed of sound and above the weather could be attained through the utilisation of B70 technology," Johnson argued. As a result of the furore two B70s survived the axe, but they cost nearly 1½ billion dollars of taxpayers' money to get into the air. They were an ominous pointer to the price of going supersonic. Johnson was right, this scale of investment could not be found from private sources and the American aircraft industry was left holding an unwanted baby. The Pentagon had abandoned its responsibility, and the only way in which a U.S. SST would come into being was either through private investment or an entirely new system of Federal funding via the FAA. In Europe this question did not even arise, because advanced industries depended on well established government procedures for funding new projects, but to many Americans such a system smacked of the evils of socialism. Quesada tried hard to impress the President that the European industries, not to mention the Soviet Union, were determined to mount a challenge, but for the Eisenhower Administration it was election year and the budget was more important than a future SST.

If Eisenhower's reaction was not enough to dampen the spirits of Quesada and the SST lobby, a Report commissioned by the FAA in 1960, and compiled by United Research Inc. of Cambridge, Massachusetts, was even more disheartening. In a thorough assessment it pointed out that even if the B70 programme was maintained, it would cost the Administration not less than one billion dollars to develop a transport version. Even more damaging was the assessment that the technical and financial risks were "greater than ever known before". The Report also suggested that there was room for only one SST to be manufactured in the free world, and so great were the risks that if the U.S. plane makers wanted to enter the race with Europe and Russia, then no single economy would be prepared to undertake the project without Government support. The report had a mixed reception: *Fortune*, the influential business magazine, remarked, "The concept challenges the imagination and at this stage almost everyone associated with aviation has good reason for being frightened of it." But it also commented "If pushing ahead with the SST is a risky proposition, the risk of not doing so may well be greater."

In Britain, scientists of the Royal Aircraft Establishment at Farnborough and the members of the STAC Committee had no such problems. They had sold their idea for an SST to the British Government in the 1950's. In commissioning preliminary work the Ministry of Aviation made a surprising choice. In addition to Hawker Siddeley, it chose the old-established company, Bristol Aircraft, to produce a design. Dr. A. E. Russell, Bristol's design chief, had been on the original STAC Committee, and his knowledge of supersonic flight tipped the scales. Bristol Aircraft were grateful for the chance to survive. As one executive confessed, "We were on the poverty line. We didn't want to starve to death." Many people thought Bristol's lucky; the Company had not had a particularly good postwar record, their Brabazon, an oversized, under-powered giant, with which the British Government had hoped to capture the long range aviation market, had been a failure. The Brabazon's successor, the turbo-prop Britannia, was a "whispering giant" which arrived too late to sell in large numbers against the American jets. But if Bristol's at that time were not the front runners in British Aviation, they had one great advantage; the firm had been experimenting with a Mach 3 fighter, known as the Bristol Type 188. It was an ugly aircraft made of stainless steel to resist the searing heat of flights above 2,000 m.p.h. Most of Bristol's experience with the T188 was painful, "it was a brute of a plane", but one lesson had emerged, the heat barrier was far more formidable than the sound barrier.

Although given total freedom by the Ministry of Supply for the feasibility study, "We could have designed a supersonic biplane, if we had been mad enough", said Dr. Russell, his team had already reached one fundamental decision.

"Supersonic speeds above Mach 2.2 were not for us. It was proving so difficult, and so expensive and the problems of the Bristol 188 were mounting with the increasing temperature. In this the T188 was absolutely crucial in making us arrive at this decision."

But Whitehall was sceptical. Ministry committees argued that the aircraft should be capable of Mach 3, and aerodynamically, a strong theoretical case could be presented. Up to the speed of sound drag increases relatively sharply, but once through the sound barrier the lift/drag ratio can be expected to be fairly constant, so that any increase in speed gives a considerable bonus in range.

This, of course, was all very encouraging in the absence of any other difficulty, but Dr. Russell knew from experience with the 188, that there was another problem; a Mach 3 plane could not be built out of aluminium alloy, because above Mach 2.2 frictional heat is so great that its crystalline structure degenerates. This was a crucial decision that made the difference between starting a practical project, using familiar and well-tried materials, or leaping into the new field of engineering required for making aeroplanes out of exotic metals. Light aluminium alloys had been used in aircraft construction for a considerable time. They were easily worked to the complex shapes and their metallurgy was well-tried. Dr. Russell plumped for an aircraft which could be built of a new aluminium alloy developed by Rolls-Royce (AU 22G) which allowed flight at speeds just above Mach 2. This was a crucial and important decision; anybody who wanted to go faster would have to master all the complex problems of titanium and stainless steel construction. It might well be possible to solve these technical problems, but could a commercial aircraft be built with the price and performance to attract the world's airlines? To ram the point

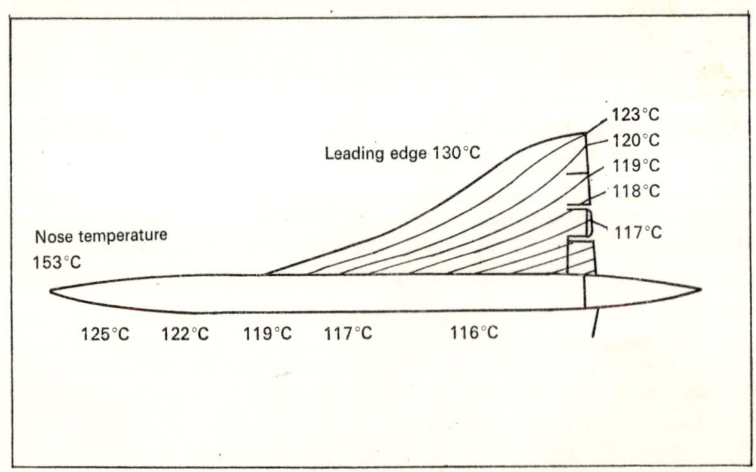

THE HEAT BARRIER
Concorde skin temperatures get hotter than boiling water at Mach 2

home, Dr. Russell's feasibility study showed that the speed advantage of a Mach 3 plane flying at over 2,000 m.p.h. across the North Atlantic was only eleven minutes over a Mach 2 plus airliner. Dr. Russell made one other important decision; he chose an existing engine.

To drive an aircraft up to a speed of Mach 2 requires engines of great power and thrust. In this Britain was fortunate in having well established companies to call on, Bristol Siddeley and Rolls-Royce. Once again Russell and his designers took a practical approach and preferred to use a known engine rather than enter a field of new technology. By a fortunate combination of circumstances, Britain was developing what was to be her last tactical bomber, the TSR 2. The aircraft promised a startling performance, even for a military aircraft. The engine powering the TSR 2 was a development of perhaps the most successful Bristol Siddeley engine, the Olympus. A turbo-jet, the Olympus had thrust a Canberra to the world altitude record, and had been proven with the R.A.F.'s Vulcan bomber. The thrust of the engine had been successively raised from 10,000 lb. initially to over 20,000 lb. The engineers believed it could be stretched much further. Rolls Royce, however, were keen to be a part of the project, and proposed a new engine to Dr. Russell. Its estimated price was to be £17 million. In the light of future experience with the RB 211, this must have been one of the most ridiculous costings ever made, even in the aircraft industry. Russell recommended the Olympus.

Bristol owes a great deal to Dr. Russell for its role as the British centre of Concorde development. Pioneer work on aircraft is not new to the city which has boasted the famous Company bearing its name since the First World War, flying string and canvas machines from nearby Filton. The airframe and associated engine companies have provided an outlet for engineering talent in the West of England; Dr. Russell is a native of Gloucestershire and Dr. Strang, who succeeded him, comes from Devon. The voices in Filton's huge Concorde assembly hangar are thick with a West Country burr redolent of the days when Bristol was one of the world's most famous ports. The soft accent contrasts markedly with the hard nasal intonation of Toulouse in South-Western France which has become the twin-city of the Concorde programme. Its past is as proud as Bristol's and it has contributed energetically to French history from the Crusades to the Resistance. The city, built of pink brick has always been known as "la ville rose" and it too was one of the earliest centres of aviation in the world. Since the war Toulouse has seen a remarkable expansion which has raised it to the fourth most important industrial centre in France. Men had been experimenting in the countryside around the "ville rose" since the early nineteenth century. The first aircraft company had opened there in 1909, and now three famous French firms were grouped around the airfield of Blagnac; Breguet, Air Fouga-Potez and Sud-Aviation (which had been nationalised in 1956). The war had been an almost total disaster for the French companies, but not quite. The British and American industries, following their huge war-time production, had the world market to themselves, but the French factories had gained some experience in maintaining Luftwaffe aircraft and designers had worked on a jet engine for the Germans—the Triton. This gave France a small launching pad from which to gain experience in gas turbine powered aircraft in 1945. The industry did not waste time. By 1950, with experience gained on research aircraft, the French companies had produced first rate fighters like the Mystere and Sud-Aviation decided to try and seize a share of the civil aviation market at one dramatic leap. It required bold designers like Pierre Satre.

"We had to make something new and original. Since we were starting from nothing, in some way we had to profit from our lateness, and as we had no projects being produced in the factory, we had to try to innovate, to lead from the front."

The Caravelle was the original aircraft produced by Sud-Aviation. It had an enormous effect on French confidence and for the first time France saw herself selling aircraft in competition with the Anglo-Saxons on the big world market.

Sud-Aviation now prepared to make another dramatic leap to build a supersonic aircraft. Their ideas were less ambitious than Bristol Aircraft's in one sense; they hoped to build a medium range aircraft which would be a natural extension of the Caravelle. The first meetings between the British and French designers were attempts to find common ground. The BAC engineers told their French colleagues—"you want to do a supersonic transport and don't know where to find the money. We want to do a supersonic transport and don't know where to find the money either. If we both use the same engine and use the same hydraulics, electrical systems and air-conditioning, we can both save money." The idea appealed to Satre, and when he returned to Sud-Aviation the practicalities were explored. But the French, even after the Agreement of 1962, took a long time to adjust to the idea that co-operation with the British meant building a common plane, not just swapping parts of a medium and long range aircraft. It took a great deal of argument before the two companies would agree to go the whole hog, but they both knew that there were other advantages in co-operation.

Gambling for Europe. *(Above)* General de Gaulle christens Concorde with a "Non" to Britain's Common Market hopes. *Elysée Palace, Paris, January 14th, 1963. (Below)* The chance that would not return. Ambassador de Courcel and Aviation Minister Amery sign the Supersonic Aircraft Agreement. *Lancaster House, London, November 29th, 1962.*

America's Paper Planes.

(Far left) Najeeb Halaby, Kennedy's "Mr. SST", Pan Am's future President. *(Left)* "The challenging new frontier in commercial aviation" President Kennedy. *U.S. Air Force Academy, Colorado Springs, June 5th, 1962.*

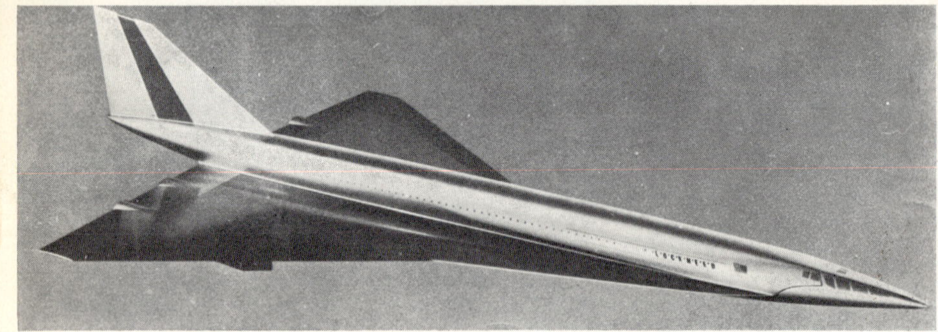

1964 SST Competition. *(Above)* Lockheed, Mach 3 with 218 passengers.

(Above) North American, Mach 2.65 with 187 passengers.
(Below) Boeing, Mach 2.7 with 150 passengers.

However brilliant the aircraft, it had to be sold to the airlines—and not only BOAC and Air France. The airlines were well aware of all the excitement about supersonic airliners. The British airlines had been on the STAC, and the aviation world can be very small. In 1961, the airline chiefs did not relish the prospect of an SST built by anybody. The arrival of the Boeing 707 and Douglas DC8 had forced them to write off sound Superconstellations and DC7s, with a great deal of service left in them. Pan American, however, had forced the pace by operating subsonic jets on the North Atlantic, cutting the flying time dramatically.

To the delight of Boeing and Douglas, every major airline had been forced to follow. The airline bosses knew it could happen again. With profits just beginning to appear after their huge investment in jets, many of the airlines were already beginning to see their balance sheets suffering from a premature arrival of the supersonics. The meeting ground of the aircraft constructors and the airlines was at the IATA Conference at Montreal in the Spring of 1961. Outside the closed doors of the Queen Elizabeth Hotel's main conference hall, notices indicated that the subject for the 14th Technical Conference was SST PROBABILITY. The feelings of the airline delegates were summed up by former IATA chief Sir William Hildred, who wondered, "Am I square in suggesting that even for the young 550 m.p.h. is not too bad? The international industry will fall back on evil days if the jets are thrust to an untimely end by the onset of the supersonic." He expressed the hope that he "would not live to see the damned thing." For six days the delegates of one hundred airlines probed every technical problem of the SST. It was a daunting new area for them, from the problems of micro-meteorites to turn-round service time; from the physical shock of supersonic travel to the sonic boom. After the Conference with reports on all conceivable aspects of supersonic flight, there was a far cooler attitude towards the SST. As the *Economist* reported—"Brash optimism has given way to something nearer humility—the airline makers are no longer trying to impress each other, but to discover precisely what they will be up against. They have not put the SST on trial so much as on the psychiatrist's couch. It is not surprising that this meeting is being held behind closed doors guarded by hotel detectives."

One new fact emerged at the Montreal Conference. The airlines and aircraft builders realised that supersonic transport would not necessarily be popular. Public opinion might actually question the technical brilliance of travelling faster than sound. A scathing attack was made on the concept by Bo Lundberg, a former test pilot and Director of the Aeronautical Research Institute of Sweden. Lundberg raised all the hazards of supersonic flight at 60,000 feet.

Would the structures of the aircraft be safe at such heights, he asked? Would there be catastrophes arising from hailstones? Would radiation have disastrous effects, particularly on pregnant women? And what about the sonic boom, surely it would be intolerable to have to live with that terrible noise? He also reminded the profit conscious airlines that the passengers had not been asked, "Whether they wish to be shot through the air rather than flown." He handed out a grim Swedish warning to the planemakers, "Supersonic transports cannot be built without introducing a host of similar features simultaneously. An aircraft designer can normally do a great deal to minimise foreseeable risks . . . but he can do nothing about the risks that he fails to foresee." The planemakers from Europe and the U.S. paid little attention to Lundberg, and wrote him off as a Nordic pessimist. They were full of confidence and ready to fight it out for the market.

Dr. Russell headed the fight for the Anglo-French project, issuing a warning to the Americans, who appeared set on a Mach 3 aircraft:

"The advocates of Mach 3 airliners seem to be confronted by a formidable array of self-inflicted difficulty. The Mach 2 solution offers close competition on similar financial arrangements to the subsonics, while the Mach 3 hotrod needs a very indulgent backer and an uninhibited operator." The American Convair engineers had an answer for this, and everyone else, it was Mach 3 or nothing because "there is some chance that the Mach 2 vehicle would be obsolescent before the first one is delivered. Faced with this outlook, few airlines are likely to buy the aircraft in fleet strength. The market would be highly speculative." The *Economist*, ever willing to offer advice to the British aircraft industry, supported the American case. "The Ministry of Aviation must be wondering whether one British company can be right and the entire American industry wrong." But as the airline bosses went home, they must have reflected long and deep on Lundberg's gloomy words.

"Once supersonic aviation has been introduced it will grow and continue to grow indefinitely if it is at all an economically sound proposition, and once introduced, but ultimately found to be a mistake because of protests from the public, it will not be possible for the airlines to turn back to pure subsonic aviation without economic disaster."

While the American, French and British engineers argued about the virtues of Mach 2 and Mach 3, another competitor had stealthily arrived—the Russians were coming. Eager to show the world that they too could build supersonic airliners, Moscow unveiled a model of an SST to be undertaken by their star aircraft designer Andrei

Tupolev. The British and French governments were surprised at its strong similarity to their own entry.

As the French and British were coming together, and the Russians had entered the field, the Americans were still vacillating about an SST. They were being dragged into the race like a "limp civil rights protestor being hauled off to jail", said Najeeb Halaby, the new director of the FAA*. But what many Americans really feared was expressed in the words of the President of American Airlines, "One of the worst beatings we'll ever get is if we have to look up to a Soviet SST, the way we had to look up to the first sputnik!"

President Kennedy had come to power in 1960, pledged to get America moving. The political consequences of being beaten by the Russians, not to mention the British and French, in launching an SST would be an enormous dent in his New Frontier image. His attitude was very different to Eisenhower's. The hopes of the American SST lobby rose. Under President Kennedy's directive they began to tackle their own new frontier in the sky "to develop the safest, most efficient and most economical aviation system attainable". Code named "Project Horizon" Halaby's SST plan reached the White House on September 5th, 1961, promising a bigger, better, faster aircraft; to be even more original than any of its rivals, it would have swing wings. But the more Halaby analysed the problems, the more snags emerged; yet the United States could not afford to fall behind. The biggest worry was how to meet the cost. Halaby started to campaign for funds from Congress, but Congress refused to believe that the Anglo-French challenge was serious. In November 1961 the President set up the Supersonic Transport Advisory Group (STAG). The Committee, answering directly to the White House, was instructed to have a final plan ready in two years. The British and French had an agreed project, and had started to cut metal in the production centres at Toulouse and Bristol by the time STAG reported in June 1963. The American airlines were becoming anxious over Washington's indecision, and Pan American Airlines resolved to take matters into its own hands. On June 4th, 1963, Juan Trippe, Pan American's President, made the dramatic announcement that he had decided to take options on six Concordes. This was an astounding piece of news. Even Air France and BOAC had not made firm commitments when Trippe acted. The American airline wanted to be at the top of the list should a viable Anglo-French aircraft emerge; this could produce a very strong marketing position on the important North Atlantic route. As *Fortune* later revealed: "This suddenly galvanised the Kennedy administration into nervous action." The White House

*The Federal Aviation Authority of the U.S.A.

tried to talk Trippe out of making a public announcement until the government was in a position to say it would proceed with the SST. The revelation added cryptically that Trippe "knowing the true state of things" decided to stand on his heels, and on June 4th, 1963, Pan American went ahead and ordered the Concorde. It has been suggested that Pan American's move was to force the U.S. government into the SST race without further delay, but whatever motivated them, the move took the President by surprise, almost as much as Concorde's makers on the other side of the Atlantic. For the first time since the war the major flag-carrier was going to purchase foreign planes. Fortunately Kennedy had a ready made chance to salvage the nation's honour; he was scheduled to speak the next day at the Air Force Academy, in Colorado Springs.

The President believed that the United States had to accept the huge challenge of building a Mach 3 SST, and that the Federal Government would have to find the dollars. The implications for American capitalism were immense. One of America's leading industries had been forced into a competitive situation by the Europeans and had to turn to the government for financial investment. The day before, the President had addressed the World Food Congress: "We have the ability, we have the means, and we have the capacity to eliminate hunger from the face of the earth". Today he was going to commit the richest nation on earth to spend billions of dollars on a risky project because of the need to satisfy national pride.

"If we can build the best operational plane of this type," he told the 40,000 young air force cadets in Falcon Stadium, "and I believe we can, then the Congress and the country should be prepared to invest the funds and the effort necessary to maintain the national lead in long range aircraft—a lead which we have held since the end of the Second World War, a lead which we should make every responsible effort to maintain." Then, he admitted that the United States had been "spurred on by the competition from across the Atlantic".

The decision on how to meet the competitive threat no longer depended entirely on the aircraft industry board-rooms. A way was open for their business and technical judgment to be vetted by the Federal Government. For the first time the United States embarked on an aircraft project for prestige rather than economic reasons. She was thinking like a European state but without well-tried political processes for carrying out such a scheme. When Kennedy took the decision he knew that the commitment could become a very heavy one for the Federal Government. The STAG report which reached the White House only days before, had contained dire warnings that the costs might grow to overwhelming proportions. In the words of one American aviation commentator: "It was a frightening dilemma—surrender our number one position in the aviation marketplace and lose face all over the world, or gamble billions at home on the assumption that American know-how and daring could build a more stupendous mousetrap, of unknown size and shape, with a technology that did not even exist. And do it in fact." The influential Senator Fulbright voiced the immediate criticism that he for one did not believe "that this nation's prestige will in any way suffer if someone else this time builds a bigger and more expensive mousetrap".

But the great paper plane race was on, and America could not afford to be left out. It remained to be seen if any would take to the air.

Sacrebleu!

3

Lorryloads of Francs

THE HOUSE OF COMMONS ratified the Anglo-French Agreement and the spending began. Julian Amery, the Minister of Aviation, had already assured sceptical Members that the price of Concorde was likely to be £150 million, rising to £170 million at the very most. Since this bill was to be shared with France, it meant that Britain would be paying approximately £9 million a year, over eight years, the expected life of the project. Compared to some of the staggering defence estimates the House had heard it seemed to be a bargain. Everyone knew that Britain could not afford to build an SST alone, but the House of Commons was suspicious of the Minister's figures for the joint venture. Her Majesty's Treasury, in particular, believed them to be in the realms of fantasy, and were known to be privately trebling the public costs. They could hardly be blamed, as so many aircraft projects had started with modest estimates in the past, and had then rocketed to a dizzy peak of expenditure. A peculiarly surrealistic game seemed to be played in Whitehall when aircraft costs were estimated, all the normal rules of accountancy being suspended. H.M. Treasury were experienced enough to see that the same game would be played with Concorde, only on a much bigger scale and this time embracing two national economies, rather than one. The decision to go ahead had, after all, been taken on a document which outlined the project in barely twenty pages: to produce a detailed estimate on what was little more than a sketch was largely a matter of guesswork. What the specification really represented was that "both sides had agreed on a shape, where the engines were to go and roughly what the plane would look like" as one of the BAC team recalled. "The silhouette was the same, but there was no agreement then as to whether it was to be a medium or long range plane, in that respect it turned out to be a stupid agreement."

The planemakers themselves believed that the decision to go ahead was "just a hard-arsed judgment". "The amount of information available at that time" in the words of one BAC engineer, "was scanty, to say the least, hardly enough to do a real estimate.

The chaps who were involved in that negotiation, knew in their own minds that the figures originally written in at the meeting stages at something around £150 million were as phoney as hell."

Macmillan's Cabinet had accepted the proposal to build a supersonic transport with few reservations. As experienced politicians who had been in government for more than a decade, they must have realised that the estimate was conveniently modest. One Minister admitted, "Well, we all thought it would cost much more than the original estimates, but I don't suppose anybody would have imagined it would have cost as much as it has." Indeed, even allowing for the rise in costs due to inflation, it is very unlikely that Macmillan's Cabinet would have started the project had they known that over ten years the bill would soar to nearly £1,000 million, and that during this time Britain would endure several sterling crises, and a damaging devaluation. At the time, however, the government believed that the £75 million was not an excessive price to pay for the future of the British aircraft industry, and a special relationship with France at the height of the Common Market negotiations.

The civil servants of the French Ministry of Finance were, perhaps, not as experienced as H.M. Treasury in costing aircraft projects, and felt very apprehensive about the magnitude of the scheme. To the Gaullist ministers, however, it seemed a bargain price for raising France's aircraft industry to world status. Above all, General de Gaulle, who regarded the civil servants of the Ministry of Finance as mere "quartermasters", wanted Concorde. After a searching interview with General André Puget, President of Sud-Aviation, he was reported as saying "Nom de Dieu nous ferons Concorde! "

As the two countries embarked upon the great enterprise they ignored Concorde's built-in cost-explosion. There were far too many unknowns. Nobody could tell how much it would require to develop the Olympus engine or a large airframe capable of supersonic flight. The designers could only guess at the allowances which had to be made for modifications and contingencies, but they could argue that Britain was starting the venture on the cheap, since considerable research had been paid for with the Bristol 188, and the Olympus engine and extensive production facilities were available at Filton.

Concorde required a new technology to take it faster than sound; it also demanded a complex bureaucracy which still operates today. Overall direction is exercised through a Directing Committee, chaired by a senior civil servant from one of the appropriate ministries in France or Britain. It is responsible for the programme as a whole and allocates Government funds. The chairmanship of this Committee passes between Britain and France every two years. It works through the Concorde Management Board, where the Chairmanship once again rotates. The main Concorde contractors are named in the Treaty, with BAC responsible for the airframe (40%), together with Sud-Aviation (60%). The engines are allocated to Rolls-Royce (60%), which has absorbed Bristol Siddeley, and to the French engine company, Snecma (40%). Concorde's organisation works through two airframe committees and two engine committees. This makes a grand total of six in all, which in turn spawn smaller specialist committees in geometric ratio embracing the eight hundred sub-contracting companies that have been involved in the project in the two countries. In terms of organisational effort alone the committees and the communications network represent a major bureaucratic achievement: but their contribution to the expedition of the project is often questioned, particularly by the men who actually build the plane. As they see it "It's a bloody miracle that the plane escaped without any humps". It is easy to see that the attendant delays in decision-making and the mountains of paper-communications have made a special contribution to the steadily rising costs and it is questionable whether the rambling bureaucracy of Concorde, lacking clear decision points, is the best way to organise Europe's biggest technological project. The French, in particular, have never been happy with the administrative structure as M. Louis Giusta, the Managing Director of Sud-Aviation, said in the Bleriot Memorial Lecture of 1969,

"Within the Manufacturers Committee of Directors, organisation has, in fact, become collegial, and this has resulted in difficult oppositions leading to delays in making decisions. Only the goodwill of individuals has made it possible to live with such an organisation."

Sir George Edwards likewise believes that the way in which the Concorde programme has been organised has led to costs being a third higher. One advantage, however, impossible to measure, has been that the endless cross-checking in committees and study groups has led to a first-rate engineering product being built with few set-backs. The double-checking eliminated errors that might otherwise have been overlooked.

Later international aerospace projects have avoided the complexity of Concorde, which, fortunately for other European schemes, has not been regarded as a model. Feeding the bureaucratic machine with vast quantities of paper, arguing for hours in committee, this has been as much a part of the price of being first with an SST, as the expense of technical research and development. It was a task the designers resented,

"The documentation we had to prepare was a public scandal, to protect the Ministers against charges by the Parliamentary Committee. Every quarter the pile of reports we had to submit were over one and a half feet thick! "

In the early days there was always plenty of room for political and industrial conflict, not always on national lines. The key job in the whole structure was Chairman of the Concorde Management Board, and the French always longed for a simple autocratic system, with the Chairman handing out directives from the summit. Georges Héreil, "Monsieur Caravelle", was very disappointed with the proposed structure. He believed that the project should have been organised in a less cumbersome way, and could not understand why the job of Chairman of the Management Board had to rotate between Britain and France. Before the Treaty was completed, he resigned the Presidency of Sud-Aviation. Some people uncharitably said it was because he could not be "Monsieur Concorde" just as he had been "Monsieur Caravelle". He became, instead, boss of Simca, the subsidiary of the giant American corporation Chrysler. His place was taken by a figure who became very popular with the British—General André Puget, an anglophile and former commander of the Free French bomber squadrons flying from Britain in the Second World War. The combination of General André Puget at the head of Sud-Aviation and Sir George Edwards as Managing Director of BAC worked extremely well. An atmosphere of mutual confidence grew up between them which was crucial at that point in Concorde's history. Sir George Edwards saw Puget's arrival as a turning point "from that time onwards I began to see hope that this joint effort would succeed." General Puget had one enormous advantage over his British colleagues. In the words of one BAC man "Whenever a problem arose, he merely picked up the ivory handled telephone and sent for another lorry-load of francs."

The two teams took time to lock together. They were drawn from very different backgrounds and training. The French technocrats were a remarkable elite, trained in the rigorous academic discipline of the École Politechnique; the British team had had a long and often rough apprenticeship with an emphasis on first hand practical experience. "We started out by being British chaps and not thumping the table hard enough." What really paid off, believes George Gedge, Managing Director of Filton Division, was "The great British capacity to compromise and give ten times more thought to understanding people. Teaching people to speak the actual language is a very small part of working together. Sitting round a table we learnt to judge the mood of a meeting by the expressions on their faces, by the way they say things, the intonations of their voices. Judging the right time to thump the table is what it's really about."

The difference in the French and English character is very great. The French distrusted the British, thinking them perfidious, wayward, materialistic, and unimaginative. The British called this "phlegm", thinking the French arrogant, inflexible and untrustworthy. Of all countries in the West likely to have difficulty in co-operating it was Britain and France, of all industries it had to be the most nationalistic, the aircraft industry. Aircraft men tend to be natural flag-wavers, so much of their work is connected with military supremacy over the foreign aggressor, or competing with him eyeball to eyeball in commercial markets. The aviation industry also has its share of extroverts, robust and confident men who speak their mind, disapproving of the diffident and introspective.

With these sort of problems the Anglo-French supersonic airliner was going to cost a great deal of money to build, even to the prototype stage. The cost, however, could be justified by a profitable market, and both countries had done their rudimentary market calculations. When the Treaty was signed France believed she could sell at least eighty of the medium range jets; Britain thought she could sell a similar number in the long-range market. American studies showed a potential market for five hundred SST aircraft, which raised European hopes. Even allowing for an American SST, the British and French estimated they could capture half of this total. But what kind of aircraft should they build to satisfy the profit conscious airlines? Throughout 1963, there was no clear answer and the Treaty itself reflected the indecision of the two Governments. Both countries had preserved their interests in writing. Article 6 stated,

"Every effort shall be made to ensure that the programme is carried out both for the airframe and for the engine, with equal attention to the medium and long range versions."

The British stuck by their requirement for a long range SST for BOAC's North Atlantic and world routes. The French wanted a medium range SST to fly over the Air France routes on which the Caravelle was doing so well. For the first year a price was paid for political indecision, and twelve months of argument elapsed before there was agreement on a single Atlantic-range plane.

The Anglo-French project had never been allowed to lose sight of its debt to the Super-Caravelle, which was planned to be a transcontinental plane for European routes expressing a peculiar Gallic view of airline markets. It was conceived in the early days before anyone talked seriously about the sonic boom. "Had they done so" in Dr. Russell's view, "the transcontinental supersonic aeroplane would have been laughed out of court at once."

It became clear that the Sud-Aviation team was determined to produce a Super-Caravelle which would have left both sides to pick up the development bill for an unwanted medium range plane. BAC, however, had been conducting tentative discussions with the airlines and after presenting the specifications to potential customers around the world it became clear that even the proposed long distance version would not have enough range, fuel reserves or passenger capacity to satisfy the market. BAC insisted on a redesign. In fact the airlines did not really want an SST in any shape or form, which exasperated some of the more enthusiastic French. "What are the major preoccupations of the airlines?" demanded General Puget, in October 1963. "To listen to them the strongest of their desires is to maintain the status quo in the technical field. Have we not heard them recently say at IATA conferences that the fact they have been obliged to re-equip would ruin them?" In general terms he was right, but the British urged caution. The commercial failures of the Comet IV and Britannia were particularly recent experiences. The two national airlines, Air France and BOAC, might be forced into buying domestic products if it were necessary to show the flag, but two airlines were an insufficient market to pay for an SST, much larger sales were needed to re-coup the huge investment. The world's airlines decisively turned the scales against the Super-Caravelle. By late 1963, they had placed no options for the plane and it was clear that the French would have to concede their medium range concept. "Really the medium range aeroplane went to bed fairly early in the project, though you can't get the French to admit it", was a BAC view. The Americans settled the Super-Caravelle late one June evening by a sudden call from New York to the Concorde sales team, which heralded an unexpected order for six aircraft from Pan American, the biggest and most important airline in the world. Anxious in case the European airlines stole a march on him, and eager to pre-empt TWA, Juan Trippe, President of Pan American, thought the £100,000 option per plane worth paying in order to share delivery of the first Concordes with Air France and BOAC. He also intended to force a decision on President Kennedy, to go forward with the American SST. At that stage options for twenty-two Concordes were lodged with BAC and Sud.

The options may have indicated a reluctant willingness by the airlines to accept an SST, but they made it quite clear that an airliner carrying less than one hundred passengers across the Atlantic would be unacceptable. The airline bosses, concerned about profitability, were prepared to play a hard game, and now that the American programme had been started, they could balance between the two projects. BOAC suddenly became a crucial weathercock of confidence in guiding other airlines on SST policy. Everybody accepted that Air France would order Concordes if instructed to do so by the French Government, but BOAC, under the Chairmanship of Sir Giles Guthrie, had staked out a position of semi-independence in the matter of aircraft purchase. BOAC had placed options for six Concordes, but Sir Giles wished to cover himself against all eventualities, particularly his North Atlantic competitors. At that stage nobody knew what the operational economics of European or American aircraft would be, but it seemed very unlikely that an airline could afford both versions. Guthrie's decision to place an option on the American version seemed to some people an unfortunate expression of no confidence in Concorde.

On 25th January, 1964, the row began when BOAC's Chairman decided to send a sales team to Washington to negotiate with the FAA for six of the future American planes, at that stage little more than projections. Coming so soon after BOAC had finally decided to opt for six Concordes, this smacked of "letting the side down", and not surprisingly the unsporting move did not find favour with the Aviation Minister, Julian Amery, whose paternal relationship to the Concorde project made him particularly sensitive to BOAC's manoeuvring. The BOAC delegation was instructed by the Minister to "take no immediate action" in Washington. Sir Giles resented this challenge to BOAC's newly won commercial freedom, and took the unusual step of publishing an answer in the airline's weekly newspaper *BOAC News* saying "The Minister, backed by the Cabinet, has written to me to make it clear that the choice of aircraft is a matter for BOAC's judgment." Pointedly he added that "if in the national interest the Government requires the Corporation to depart from commercial interests, the Minister will give a written directive which in effect will absolve BOAC from the responsibility of any losses which might ensue." A week later in the House of Commons Julian Amery gave in effect his reply, "It is important that on this project, as indeed on others, we should not go out of our way, as some critics so often do, to run down British projects which are doing very well." This was met with patriotic outbursts of cheering from the Government benches as the Minister continued, "The terms on which BOAC will finally make up their minds must be a matter for their commercial judgment, of course", and putting BOAC firmly in their place, he added "in consultation with me! " The Minister had made his point and everything was smoothed over. A week later BOAC's commercial judgment was endorsed when they announced options on six American SSTs because the two aircraft appeared to be "complementary to each other rather than directly competitive."

Across the Atlantic, the American SST, although even less well-defined than Concorde, was doing very good business. The reputation of the American constructors was so formidable that the world's airlines were prepared to order straight from the drawing board. In 1964 orders were standing at almost two for the American jet (63), against every one for Concorde (37). But President Kennedy's project had run into stiff opposition in Congress, foreshadowing the difficulties to come. The plan for financing the whole project through government-backed Federal aid was proving unpopular and thought by some to be "un-American". Already the scheme for joint financial participation between Government and industry was dragging through a series of committee hearings to determine precisely how much each side should pay. The Administration's main objective was to beat the Europeans, and they believed they stood the best chance of getting the vital world beating design from a competition. The leading American companies —Lockheed, North American, Convair and Boeing, set to work on their drawing boards, knowing that a billion-dollar development programme was at stake. Najeeb Halaby, the head of the FAA, summoned the airlines to Washington and confidently told them the "American SST will be in commercial service not more than six months after Concorde is flying paying passengers." The airlines seemed to agree when, according to *Fortune*, Halaby had "briskly drummed up bids for a non-existent production line, dropping the admission price to one hundred thousand dollars." TWA beat Pan American by a few hours. Still smarting from their defeat, Pan American hurried their downpayment to the FAA with a note to the effect that "Our bankers' check in the amount of $1,500,000 in favour of the USA is enclosed."

When Kennedy took the decision Congress was anxious about the cost. In the Senate there was more than a little worry that the project was uneconomic. The American manufacturers, knowing the cost of building a supersonic airliner, would not undertake the work without Federal Government financial assistance. How much help the Administration would provide was argued intensely in Washington. At first the White House wanted manufacturers to pay a third of development costs, with airlines and users contributing another third, the government paying the rest. After lobbying and argument the manufacturers' proposed contribution slipped from a third to a ninth. A start had to be made somewhere and, determined to get things moving, Kennedy called upon Congress to vote sixty million dollars so that a team could be brought together under FAA leadership, but the Administration ran into tough Senate opposition, led by a certain Senator William Proxmire from

Wisconsin. A Democrat and an astute politician, he tried to strike out the sixty million dollars on the grounds that it was "subtle nationalisation" of the aircraft industry. "We don't want to move in the direction the British and French have moved" he said. Striking at the deepest roots of capitalism was what he feared. "We don't want to nationalise our corporations." This spectre of insidious "nationalisation" was to bedevil the American SST programme, which had found an implacable enemy in Senator Proxmire, who failed in his first attack. Two days later President Kennedy, the great advocate of an American SST, was assassinated. A shadow fell over the enterprise.

Lyndon B. Johnson's first briefing on the American supersonic transport was the Black Osborne Report, which all but pulled the rug from under Halaby's carefully laid plans at the FAA. Eugene Black, former President of the World Bank, had taken a cold economist's view of the project in a report specially commissioned by the Administration. He reminded the President of the enormity of the programme. "Never before will such vast sums have been invested in capital facilities, development costs and production financing just to produce a commercial aircraft. If our nation is not willing to face the issue financially, technologically or managerially, we would strongly recommend dropping the programme now." The Report then warned against tying the American programme too closely to Concorde. Referring to the proposed project as a "financial and technical gamble of such proportions that we cannot possibly recommend it" the Report went on to propose that the SST should be delayed for another decade. Its conclusions were that it was already too late to launch a crash programme to stop the Concorde; that the Europeans would cream the market, with the United States suffering a painful loss of prestige at not winning the race. It was President Johnson's moment of decision—the "go" or "no go" point. His views had not changed since he had fought for the B70 bomber, as the precursor of an SST. He chose to stay in the game; American manufacturers were invited to press on with the competition.

When their entries appeared in January 1964, they were predictably vague. North American had sketched in windows on a larger version of their B70 bomber; Lockheed produced a delta plane that looked like a big brother to Concorde and Boeing had latched on to the "swing wing" idea that was contained in the Project Horizon report. All were to carry nearly twice Concorde's number of passengers and were much faster, but none could satisfy the Black Osborne criteria over economic operation. A committee, under Robert MacNamara, vetted the plans in the Spring. The likeliest looking airframes and engines were chosen, and the teams sent back to the drawing board for a re-think.

In London the "ominous silence" which had noticeably descended over BAC was rudely shattered by the outspoken criticisms of the Concorde's finances emerging from the House of Commons' financial watchdog, the Committee of Public Estimates. This committee had the responsibility of checking public spending. Their criticism was painful and embarrassing for the Government. The cost of £150 million was found to be speculative. The Treasury was accused of being derelict in its duty, through not involving itself in the Treaty terms. The Committee disapproved of the way in which the Government had entered the project; it was,

"An example of executive action which commits Parliament to an unspecified heavy expenditure on a project on which the returns must be problematical." There was also anxiety about the open-ended nature of the commitment. There was no break clause. In its report the Committee said,

"A form of break clause would have been an entirely natural and proper section to incorporate into an agreement which commits Parliament to so heavy a financial burden in the next decade." Neil Marten, the Parliamentary Secretary to the Ministry of Aviation, disagreed with the Committee, describing the Treaty as "a sound, sensible and far-sighted document."

This was all very well, but the Cabinet were only too pleased to have a contract without break clauses, there was always the fear that France would be perfidious rather than Albion. In the view of one of Macmillan's Cabinet Ministers—"I don't think anybody would have gone into a project like that at the time if the other party could get out of it."

A major row was clearly brewing over costs. When a question was asked in Parliament about the "awful gap", the Chancellor passed the buck to Amery who was responsible for the financial management of the project. The Minister countered by saying that financial control was available. "I do not think the budget has been exceeded so far" he said. He knew, however, that extensive modifications were taking place, and was prepared to allow that "the only question is whether the modifications taking place to the engine and wing structure may put something on the estimate."

Months of continuous argument between BAC and Sud-Aviation were having an effect at last, a joint aircraft was emerging. The results of the wind tunnel tests, airline requirements and hundreds of committee papers at all levels had now, finally, persuaded the French to change their mind about the desirability of building a larger aircraft with greater engine power. Agreement was

The Battle for Concorde. *(Above)* Britain's Aviation Minister Roy Jenkins confronts French Transport Minister Jacquet, "A boot-faced reception." *Paris, October 29th, 1964. (Below)* Defeat and reconciliation: Wilson and Brown meet the General. *January 1967.*

(Above) Dr. A. E. Russell ("Russ"): Bulldog, Blenheim, Brabazon, Britannia, T.188. *(Below)* Pierre Satre: Armagnac, Caravelle.

(Above) Sir George Edwards ("Uncle"): Managing Director BAC. *(Below)* General André Puget: President, Sud-Aviation, 1962-1966.

(Above) Dr. W. J. Strang: T.188. *(Below)* Lucien Servanty: Armagnac, Caravelle.

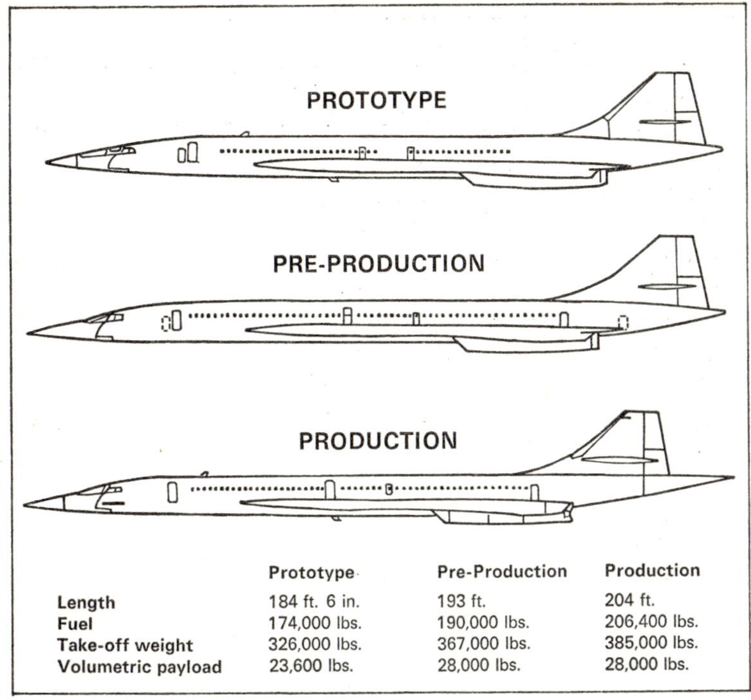

	Prototype	Pre-Production	Production
Length	184 ft. 6 in.	193 ft.	204 ft.
Fuel	174,000 lbs.	190,000 lbs.	206,400 lbs.
Take-off weight	326,000 lbs.	367,000 lbs.	385,000 lbs.
Volumetric payload	23,600 lbs.	28,000 lbs.	28,000 lbs.

THE THREE CONCORDES

A longer body, bigger wings and more payload are the result of nine years' development.

reached in March 1964—nineteen months after the Treaty was signed—that the Concorde was finally going to be an Atlantic-range plane. It is hardly an exaggeration to add the first hand comment of one BAC engineer "On a big issue it takes the Frenchman about three years to admit that he has got it wrong."

The combined efforts of BAC and Sud were now directed towards showing the politicians and a sceptical press that a market really did exist, and selling the Concorde. Full of confidence, the joint Anglo-French team embarked on a selling campaign at the IATA technical committee to be held at Beirut in 1964, armed with the new computerised facts and details. Although they were working together on Concorde, however, the old Anglo-French rivalry was under the surface. BAC and Sud were deadly competitors when it came to selling their own separate national products; BAC were selling the new medium range "111" directly against the Caravelle. The world's airlines might be the customers for Concorde tomorrow, they were more immediate customers for the "111" and the Caravelle. In the Mediterranean evenings the BAC members of the sales team infiltrated the plush corridors of Beirut's luxury hotels armed with "111" brochures for the airline bosses, should they feel in need of bed-time reading. But in the conference hall, the Anglo-French team pulled together and presented details of the new Concorde. It was to be a bigger plane: fourteen feet longer; wing area up 15%; weight up to 326,000 lb. and most important of all, it was going to fly 118 passengers 4,000 miles. To do this a price had to be paid—the engines were going to be re-designed to increase the power. Moreover, it was going to be in service by 1971 and make its first flight in 1967. Confidently the two companies projected their plane as a "sensible and practical extension of present day knowledge". In a clear reference to the problematical new materials of the American SST "we are using materials and methods which have been proven. . . . We are not going beyond the state of the art and for those reasons both our aeroplane and our timetable are realistic."

In order to get the prototype into the air the two Governments would have to agree to the "something on the estimates". Money had to be found for the re-designed Olympus 593 engine, and modification to the airframe, after nearly a year had been lost in argument. Everyone knew that Amery's initial figure of £150-£170 million could hardly cover all these changes. The British Treasury had taken Parliament's criticism about its lack of control to heart. In the summer of 1964, just how well the Treasury had actually carried out its duties was revealed when the Aviation Minister came to answer three straightforward questions on the Commons Order Paper on July 9th. Having just returned from meeting the French Minister in Paris, where the new figures for the re-designed Concorde had been agreed, Members found it highly suspicious that the bland replies on the project's progress made no mention of cost. Scenting a hare of considerable proportions, the hounds of the Parliamentary Labour Party leapt to the chase. Mr. Cronin asked the Minister "Would he give the latest estimate?" Unexpectedly at bay, the Minister replied in a low and seemingly disinterested voice that Britain's share would be "something like £140 million." A gasp of astonishment swept across the Opposition benches. Even the Government bench swallowed hard. The total bill had doubled to almost £300 million. In the words of *The Times* "Mr. Amery had caught them utterly off their guard, and before the questions on every lip could even be framed, the House had passed on to the next business. Only the Labour spokesman on aviation was quick enough to get in one small query 'How long had the Minister known that the cost would be almost double the original estimate?'

" 'Since last weekend', Mr. Amery replied suavely."

"Nothing is being left to chance—we even have a team working on the most advantageous time to cancel."

4

Non!

On Monday, October 19th, 1964, Harold Wilson's newly returned Labour Cabinet took the decision to scrap Concorde. It was the new Government's first Cabinet meeting, and according to one of the Ministers, one of its first decisions. Two years after the Anglo-French Agreement, this was to be Concorde's most serious crisis. It is ironic that it should have fallen to Harold Wilson to make the decision, since the new Prime Minister had argued powerfully for a "white-hot" British technology in his address to the Labour Party Conference in 1963.

After victory at the polls, it was the heat of a financial crisis which wilted the Election promises of the new team. Within twenty-four hours of taking office, the new Prime Minister was presented with what he called a "formidable Treasury memorandum that Britain was facing a deficit of £800 million on her overseas payments for 1964 and a scarcely less daunting prospect for 1965." There was a run on the pound and the Prime Minister was under considerable pressure to severely cut government spending. Night after night, he had to listen to the country's bankers urging "immediate cuts in government expenditure" that would have meant "half-finished roads left as an eyesore on the countryside, schools left without a roof", in the Prime Minister's view sacrificing welfare policies to "satisfy a foreign financial fetishism".

Harold Wilson had been returned as a Socialist Prime Minister and his intention was to defend the country's social policies rather than continue with an expensive project which was showing unmistakable signs of runaway cost-escalation. The Labour Members at Westminster had no love for Concorde, which many regarded as a Tory prestige project. The part Duncan Sandys and Julian Amery had played in starting the whole scheme had earned it the tag of "a Macmillan family affair". One pro-Concorde Labour M.P. felt that this must have influenced the cancellation decision. "Concorde was always regarded as Amery's pet" he said. "Amery was a very unpopular man with the Labour Front Bench. I think the idea of killing his project gave some people a lot of unconscious pleasure." Also playing a part in questioning Concorde was an Aviation Consultant called Richard Worcester, who had been highly thought of as "a shy retiring man with a brilliant insight into aviation problems" by one of Mr. Wilson's key advisers. He had been circulating a number of influential Labour M.P.s with information and analysis since 1963. In the aviation industry itself, Mr. Worcester's weekly newsheet modelled on the influential American *Aviation Weekly* was not credited with quite the same authority. "We read it when we wanted to balance our own enthusiastic predictions" said one BAC executive. Worcester was convinced that Concorde would be outstripped by the bigger and better American SST, and that it could not survive as a commercial proposition. More to the point was the fact that the Conservative Government had been pouring more than half Britain's total scientific research and development budget into the aviation industry. The costs of the tactical bomber TSR2 were rocketing up and it was absorbing nearly a million pounds a week at the time of the 1964 Election. Even the Conservatives were anxious. In the Tory marginal seats, like that of Aviation Minister Julian Amery, many of which happened to contain large aircraft factories, it was not surprising that any whispers of forthcoming cuts contemplated by the Conservative Government were kept in the deepest recesses of Whitehall.

Once in office, the financial situation left the Prime Minister with little choice; he had to act quickly. It was to be the first time that Britain's sick economy became a factor in Concorde, and it would continue as the major threat throughout the life of the Labour Government. The new Administration badly wanted to put its promises of "getting Britain going" into action. Money was needed in other directions—the re-structuring of industry, more modest technological projects and social welfare; something would have to be cut to pay for these, and Concorde, with all its Tory associations, was top of the list. It stayed there for six years. Only one thing saved it—the terms of the Treaty. The Prime Minister had a good case for cancellation apart from the sterling problems; the bill had already risen from £150 million to £280 million, and was expected to go higher as a result of fresh improvements to the engines and airframe, decided upon by the constructors.

The Government's plans were hurriedly formulated in a White Paper submitted to the first Cabinet by the new Minister for Economic Affairs, George Brown. In what later came to be dubbed the "Brown Paper", Clause 13, sub-section 6, firmly labelled Concorde "A prestige project" and marked it down for urgent re-examination, a polite euphemism for cancellation, but it was not really as premeditated as it appeared. In the words of one Cabinet Minister,

"We had reached the very broad decision before we came into office to re-allocate expenditure. It was a mistake to think that the Government was specifically anti-Concorde. It was George Brown's rhetoric, illuminating a perfectly clear enonomic decision about priorities. When looking for something to describe as a prestige project, Concorde was the obvious choice. It was as simple as that." Even in the face of continuing Treasury and Bank of England pressure to prune Government expenditure, sacrificing Concorde proved far harder than any of the Ministers had realised. They thought the coffin had been nailed down on their first morning in power. The attempt failed largely through inexpert diplomacy and it left Concorde hanging round the neck of Mr. Wilson's Government like an albatross which defied all later efforts to cast it aside. The haste with which the British Government rushed into the cancellation attempt left no time for a full evaluation of the consequences. Apart from the likely effect on the aircraft industry, Britain's reputation as a business and engineering country were at stake, together with the jobs of thousands of workers. Diplomatic relations with France and Europe were jeopardised, because the Government in its enthusiasm to rid itself of Concorde had, apparently, overlooked one simple fact—that there was no break clause in the Anglo-French Agreement. A fact that had been plainly publicised by the House of Commons Estimates Committee only a few months previously. In a strange twist of fate, it was the Conservative Government's admitted defence against untimely French withdrawal that trapped the Labour Government. If Wilson wanted to axe Concorde, he must first persuade de Gaulle to abandon his cherished scheme to end "American colonisation of the skies".

The news broke ominously in Paris during a meeting of the Conseil des Ministres that the British Government wanted to re-examine Concorde, which the British press were interpreting as cancellation. Monsieur Peyrefitte, the Minister of Information, tersely announced, "It's a matter of a greatly increased burden which will be discussed between the two countries." The French clearly intended that the burden should be placed squarely on the British Prime Minister's shoulders. The French Government received very little warning. Although the Brown Paper's one specific proposal for Government economy implied that negotiations were already under way, "The Government have already communicated with the French Government their wish to re-examine urgently the Concorde project"—they were not, in fact, begun until the Saturday afternoon two days before publication, when the document was already in the tight security of the Government printers. The *Sunday Times* was later to disclose a bizarre sequence of diplomatic diversions.

"Sir Pierson Dixon, the British Ambassador in Paris, had been invited to shoot with, of all people, Maurice Heurtreux, the Chairman of the French aero-engine company Hispano Suiza. Half way through the drive, a harassed official from the British Embassy drove up in a cloud of dust and summoned Dixon back to the Embassy; a matter of the greatest urgency had suddenly come up. When Dixon got back to the Rue du Faubourg St. Honoré, he found that Concorde was to be killed. Would he please inform Couve de Murville immediately? Unfortunately it was not as easy as all that. It was not until Sunday evening, by which time he had missed part of another shoot, that Dixon was able to break the news to officials at the Quai d'Orsay."

The French Government, responsible for a half share of the £280 million project, were not the only ones left in the dark. Even the unfortunate Roy Jenkins, Minister of Aviation, had not been told, and he was the man who would have to take on the unenviable job of officially telling the French, and clearing up the mess. He was not yet a member of the Cabinet, and only learnt of it, in true Westminster style, from Sir Richard Way at Brook's Club in St. James's.

Least of all were the manufacturers told. They too discovered in the classic way. A journalist from a Sunday newspaper telephoned BAC headquarters on the Saturday after the Cabinet meeting. Sir George Edwards lost no time in contacting his senior executives, most of whom were on a BAC 111 sales mission in the United States. A transatlantic telephone call to a Dallas motel brought them the stunning news. "Once the Labour Government was returned we knew TSR2 was a dead duck" confessed one of the BAC men. "We just didn't see Concorde coming." If Concorde were to be cancelled as well as its military project TSR2, BAC's management knew that a massive blow would be dealt to the company, meaning the end of its Filton division, putting thousands of workers out of a job. But as the team set off immediately for London and crisis meetings, trying to snatch British Sunday papers en route in unlikely places like Chicago, Sir George Edwards was assembling more information. Thirty-six hours later, when they arrived in his office, as one remembers "He waved the Brown Paper at me and said, 'There you are, we've had the Concorde'."

The French were very tight-lipped about the news of Harold Wilson's decision. But four days later several French newspapers were suggesting that Federal Germany was ready to take up the responsibility in the event of "British defection". On October 28th, Roy Jenkins flew to Paris to meet his opposite number, M. Jacquet, with the Cabinet's instructions to get out of Concorde. The "negotiations" amounted to little more than thirty-five minutes of embarrassed discussion. According to well placed leaks in the French press he had outlined a number of alternatives for the continuation of Concorde,

1. Limitation of all agreements between Sud-Aviation and BAC to the construction of prototypes.
2. Formation of a European consortium of six or seven states to share the burden, or as an alternative—Britain, France and the U.S.A. to work together.
3. Stretching out the production time of the first four Concordes.
4. France would undertake to install and finance the assembly lines herself.

The French were highly suspicious and suspected a deal between Britain and the U.S. on the SST, particularly in view of Britain's sterling problems. The French position was uncompromising. Jacquet pointed to the Treaty and reminded Jenkins that there was no escape clause. According to one member of the BAC board, who was, perhaps not surprisingly, in Paris at the time,

"He got a pretty 'boot-faced' reception from the French who referred him to the terms of the agreement signed in November 1962 and showed not the slightest inclination to be helpful."

On his return to London it was Mr. Jenkins' turn to be "boot-faced" when he addressed the inevitable press conference at London Airport. The French he explained had listened "carefully and sympathetically". . . . "I did not expect them to commit themselves and they did not do so." He explained that the British Government wanted an urgent review because of the "economic situation at home" and because it had "grave doubts about the economic viability of the plane". He then went on, "If we are convinced that the investment in the Concorde from our point of view and from the French point of view would help us pay our way in the world consistent with the amount of money spent on it, then, of course, we would have to go ahead; but at the moment we have our doubts." The French had been left in no doubts that the British Government, if it had its own way, would cancel the aircraft immediately, and so they calmly decided to sit tight and let Mr. Wilson sweat it out.

On November 6th, Her Majesty's Opposition called for a full-fledged government inquiry. Letters poured into *The Times* with deep concern being expressed for "the youth of this country and the young technologists" who would "regard the cancellation of the Concorde as a sign that there is little future for advanced technology in this country". It was even speculated that should the project founder "it may be anticipated that the French would look to the Americans to take our place". One correspondent asked, "Is it not worthwhile subsidising the Concorde venture (which may, after all, turn out to be a money-making success), and thus ensure our remaining a leading aviation nation?" The long-standing critics of the Concorde lost no time in urging the Government to stand firm; "We'll lose a plane nobody wants and gain a new world" trumpeted the *New Statesman*, conjuring up tempting visions of automatic cars, high speed transport and what they called "social automation rather than military or aircraft gadgetery".

If the debate was pitching to a hysterical level in public, behind the scenes the aircraft industry was using every method to remind Ministers of the realities of cancellation. Sir George Edwards left the Minister in no doubt that BAC would be forced to close its Filton plant, with a damaging effect on Bristol and the South West. The Government began to waver. A significant leader in the *New Statesman*, with its connections inside the Labour Party, reflected the backtracking going on in Downing Street.

"Mr. Jenkins broods on international co-operation in advanced technology, and his advisers are considering whether an economic return can be expected from a project which costs so much. Allied to the problems of economics and technology is the less calculable one of diplomacy, and that hinges on the kind of relations Mr. Wilson's Government wants with de Gaulle. . . . Should Concorde be scrapped, the diplomatic consequences would be considerable and these are being taken seriously by the government."

If Mr. Wilson's team had been trapped by their inexperience of diplomacy, Charles de Gaulle left no manoeuvre untried to prevent them wriggling out of the contract, determined to save France's technological *gloire*. A "European Plan" was formulated and Sweden, Germany, Holland and Belgium were approached to see whether they would help finance the project if Britain withdrew. Conveniently the Soviet Foreign Trade Minister, Mr. Patolichev was in Paris for the Franco-Soviet Trade Agreement and rumours that Russia was to supply replacement engines were carefully leaked by the Gaullist press. Only a solitary note of support for Harold Wilson came from de Gaulle's old rival, M. Gaston Deferre, the Mayor of Marseilles, who in a letter in "Le Provençal" asked "if it is unreasonable to complain that the British are thinking of abandoning the project when General de Gaulle slammed the door on them in January 1963." But almost all the French press were against the British move to cancel. M. Jean-Jacques Servan-Schreiber, who was sympathetic with British problems, turned on Mr. Wilson for behaving like General de Gaulle,

"However good the British arguments may be for suppressing Concorde, it is unacceptable that a unilateral decision should be taken without consulting the partners, and that associates should be faced with a fait accompli. . . . The consequences, in every respect, of the behaviour will cost them, and even purely financially, much more than the saving on Concorde. That is the Gaullist method" warned M. Servan-Schreiber. "We have denounced it too often in France to be indulgent with British Socialists."

Events reached the point of decision. On November 19th, at the Conseil de Ministres at the Elysée, President de Gaulle called for a report on "the machine". M. Jacquet gave a progress report, and after a discussion, according to witnesses, the French government sent a message to London based on three points—

1. The original Agreement between Britain and France did not allow any revision.
2. To delay the production of the aircraft would be commercially dangerous and allow the Americans to catch up.
3. In its re-designed, transcontinental shape, Concorde must be built, as planned.

Harold Wilson was on the hook. He either accepted the French position and went ahead with Concorde as the Conservative government had planned, or he ruptured the Treaty, and risked the humiliation of an international law-suit with Gaullist France.

At this point the Attorney General's (Sir Elwyn Jones) legal opinion was crucial. In his view the Treaty would allow the French government to sue Britain for a sum not far short of £100 million in the event of a British withdrawal from the project. There was little doubt that de Gaulle would do this if pressed. The Cabinet's previously firm resolve crumbled. "Cabinets blanch a bit at legal opinions" was the reaction of a Minister whose resolve never weakened. "With hindsight, of course, we can now see that even if the Attorney General's legal opinion was correct, our maximum liability would have been trifling compared with the expenditure to which we are now committed." By no means all international lawyers were convinced that France would have a watertight case to present to the Hague Court. The term that "Every effort shall be made to ensure that the programme is carried out . . ." might give an arguable loophole. The Government covered the retreat. Pressed in the House of Commons by a pro-Concorde Labour backbencher to give an answer on the aircraft's future a week later, Mr. Jenkins gave a masterful display.

Mr. Edelman: "Has the Minister noted the view of both partners in the Anglo-French project that cancellation will not only cause heavy financial losses but also incalculable losses of goodwill? Is he now prepared to say that it is the Government's intention to proceed with this project in one way or another?"

Mr. Jenkins: "No. But we are hopeful of coming to amicable arrangements with the French Government. I am sure that my hon. friend, who is a great believer in Anglo-French collaboration, will do everything he can to help in this respect. We are discussing this with the French Government, and the nature of our discussion is strictly confidential."

Pressed further by a Conservative member for an assurance that the Minister "will not come to a decision which is not amicably arranged with the French Government", Mr. Jenkins replied laconically—

"Amicability is necessarily a two way process, but I remain hopeful." But in the House of Lords, the Government spokesman, Lord Shackleton, was able to assure their Lordships "I must with complete honesty say that I have not heard that word 'cancellation' used in the discussions." The French and most of the British press took this with a large pinch of salt.

Although certain members of Mr. Wilson's Cabinet might well argue to cancel and be damned, others were not prepared to take the risks. The Government opted for a compromise solution; the French must be persuaded to at least slow down the programme. But having suffered one diplomatic reverse the British Government were in a weak position, and General de Gaulle knew it. The French refused to discuss Concorde at all unless they received a categorical guarantee that the British would observe the Treaty and build the plane. The weeks passed in increasing frustration, in the factories work was grinding to a standstill and the December meeting of officials which was to discuss, ironically, ways of cutting down the investment, was called off.

The Ministry and BAC proposed a compromise. The so-called "knife and fork solutions" began to emerge for slowing down the rate of investment and uncoupling the prototype programme from the decision to tool up for production. This meant that the prototypes would be hand-built without full production jigs. The BAC costs department produced sets of figures for six different combinations of compromise. To the Labour Government this looked like "cancellation with honour" but the problem was how to interest the French.

Then came intervention from an unexpected direction. For weeks as the crisis raged, work at Filton and Toulouse had dwindled to almost nothing, and the workers had begun to get anxious. Even the senior executives did not speak to each other officially. The anxiety of the workers grew and their union leaders took steps to protect them. They acted internationally. An old Socialist militant, Eugène Montel, who had been a colleague of Léon Blum, and was a Deputy for Toulouse, arrived in London to lobby the British Labour Party on behalf of the unions. On the British side Clive Jenkins intervened and flew twice to Paris for meetings with his opposite number to bring pressure to bear on the French Government for a compromise.

These dramatic excursions contributed to easing the situation. Both sides were becoming worried about the indecision. The British Government drifted to an uneasy acceptance that Concorde would continue. The newly born Ministry of Technology, and its ex-union chief, Frank Cousins, who was now responsible for Concorde, had been steadily won round by technological arguments. By Christmas it was becoming clear that Concorde could not be cancelled, and the Cabinet turned its attention to the military TSR2, costing an enormous sum and unprotected by de Gaulle. Lord Plowden was commissioned to assess the British aircraft industry's future. He recommended joint projects with Europe which helped Concorde but gave an excuse for cancelling TSR2. In 1965 work picked up again at Filton with the Government playing Concorde empirically.

It was still hoped that there would be opportunities to escape and it was the constant search for these chances that made the weight of the costly albatross particularly heavy at times of financial crisis. The shooting had stopped, and workers and management at the BAC factories climbed out of their slit trenches and got on with the project. For the first time in the ten-week crisis the two managements were allowed to make direct contact. To the senior executives of Sud-Aviation who were always trying to convince their Anglo-Saxon partners that the great English triumphs, Agincourt, Cressy,

Trafalgar, were French losses rather than English victories, Charles de Gaulle's victorious Concorde must have given cause for satisfaction. If nothing else, they were now a team, fighting on the same side and bloodied in battle. In Dr. Russell's view "It was the time when we got really friendly, we rallied together. It helped relations enormously."

The New Year saw Concorde begin to take shape as the large sub-assemblies were brought together on each side of the Channel. It was no longer a paper plane, unlike its American rival. One American Aviation Consultant with the FAA, John Hoving, was not the only person disappointed with progress, "I am struck, as a matter of fact, by an anomaly that seems to run through the whole supersonic program: committees, groups, flip-chart artists all going on and on and on, assembling an immense amount of paper. What I am assuming is that they will fly a paper aeroplane off the FAA roof one day, with or without the sonic boom." There were storm signals for the American SST. In the middle of the Concorde crisis, a British Treasury team had arrived in Washington, under Sir Eric Roll, to canvass U.S. Administration support for the pound. When Sir Eric disclosed the Government intentions in the "Brown Paper" about Concorde, the U.S. Treasury members might have wished that they could have disposed of their supersonic plane with such ease.

To get America's SST moving, the Pentagon advised the President to recruit a military man to run the FAA. Najeeb Halaby, shortly to take over from Juan Trippe at Pan American, was replaced by General McKee. Congress objected. It wanted a civilian, and what was more irksome, with his retirement pension and FAA salary, McKee would be earning more than anyone except the President and Vice-President of the United States, but the General was installed in June, and promptly confirmed Congress's worst fears by demanding a further 180 million dollars for the project. *Aviation Daily* accused the Secretary of Defense:

"In essence there has been nothing going for the program, as far as the industry and the public have been concerned, but press releases —and they have been few and far between since the program was dropped into Secretary McNamara's lap." The military took a firmer grip on the FAA programme when General Maxwell took the post as General McKee's deputy. To some shrewd observers it looked as though the Pentagon was going to get a supersonic bomber by the "back door". This was not discounted by Maxwell saying, "Anybody can use it. If I can haul garbage supersonically then the garbage people will buy it. If the aeroplane is as good as we're saying it is, it will have an application on some of their missions." This was greeted as welcome fodder by the growing anti-SST lobby, who discerned the influence of the American industrial-military complex behind the scheme.

In the Spring of 1965, with the feared American plane still on paper, the atmosphere between the British and French governments improved. To some extent the confusion in Washington certainly helped. In spite of initial reservations Roy Jenkins was sounding positively enthusiastic, "We are anxious to get the market and therefore an important factor is how close the Americans are behind us. Compatible with getting a market, we don't want to rush into a decision without due consideration. We are determined not to spend the money to lose the market." The "due consideration" which the Minister guardedly mentioned, was yet another re-design of the aircraft, which of course would mean more money.

The direct pressure for a re-design came from the airlines, who demanded still more seats and improved economics. If Britain was to persevere with the scheme then it became vital to interest more customers in Concorde. The plane now being built was the plane of the Beirut IATA summit, with one hundred and eighteen seats, and scheduled for service in 1971, but now that the Americans were flagging there was time to boost Concorde's customer appeal. It was decided to build the prototypes according to the agreed design to gain valuable flying experience, but to incorporate changes in the next aircraft. According to Dr. Strang the changes in design arose from airline intervention. "It was really spearheaded by the Pan American representatives who pressed for, and got adopted, a further lengthening of the fuselage and a rearrangement of access doors. They wanted an increase in volumetric capacity and we gave them another seven feet and up to one hundred and forty seats."

It is a measure of the skill of the BAC-Sud design teams that they achieved this increase in capacity by exploiting the aerodynamics of the sharp-edged delta, once again vindicating its original choice. By changing the camber and curl on the wing-tips greater area was achieved without increasing the span, but at the same time improving the lift. Inevitably the aircraft's weight rose—this time to 350,000 lbs, but the changes were not achieved without the inevitable battle to convince the French of the necessity for making them. After a considerable battle, led by Dr. Russell, the Concorde Directing Committee had to issue a directive ordering the design alterations to be made.

The Concorde might now possess more appeal, but the real proof would be orders from the airlines. When Roy Jenkins gave his approval to the new design, he must also have appreciated that the costs would rise.

Concorde had survived its biggest crisis, saved by de Gaulle insisting on Britain's Treaty obligations. But the war against the SST went on, led by the *Economist*. Its aviation correspondent, Mary Goldring, the scourge of the aircraft engineers, was not taken in. She angrily protested.

"Someone must call the bluff; the Concorde supersonic airliner will not be built." Suggesting confidential information from the top of BAC she announced, "This is no sourpuss guess; it is the consensus of opinion among the men closely connected with the project." The leader in the *Economist* of July 31st, 1965, attacked stridently—"And yet the charade goes on; another round of sour criticism, another week of cuts in Government spending and Concorde—officially—still survives. Unofficially, most people have written it off as dead." Labelling Concorde as a "bad aircraft", she pointed out that "Extreme American caution, despite huge resources, despite careful research, should be a warning that supersonic airliners that can pay their way are not things designed on the back of an envelope." She ended by asking in exasperation: "Has everyone, every political party lost his tongue? . . . Have they all constituents in Bristol?" Perhaps she should have asked whether they all had had to cope with General de Gaulle in the Elysée.

5

The Gentle Sound of Thunder

On a damp April morning in 1965 a small crowd collected on a rugby field on the windswept flatlands of Huntingdonshire. It was a strange rural meeting of journalists, M.P.s, airline officials and aircraft engineers, leavened with the occasional "man from the Ministry". Roy Jenkins, the Minister of Aviation, arrived and the audience was ushered into the temporary stands by officials who handed out cards to everyone. As everybody waited expectantly for something to happen it could have been a meeting of the local point to point. This was the Ministry of Aviation's first public demonstration of the phenomenon known as sonic boom. The audience was to be treated to a concert of "bangs", some artificial, some produced by letting off small explosive charges, and others created by the "real thing"—shining RAF Lightning fighters thundering overhead. The object of the exercise was to simulate a Concorde-size sonic boom and as the bangs blasted overhead, the audience noted reactions on the Ministry's specially printed card, "Rather like a loud shotgun" wrote one journalist; another—"the booms were softer than the maroons used to call out the Padstow lifeboat." In the deafening silence that followed, Roy Jenkins gave a press conference, where he was guardedly non-committal over the precise nature of Concorde's likely boom, but hoped that it would produce a pressure of 2 lb. per square foot—less than many of the booms which had cracked the visitors' ear-drums that morning.

The local population were not quite so happy. The RAF received eight calls of complaint, but a scientist who had monitored the tests with delicate electronic instruments set amongst the tomato plants in a local greenhouse, assured reporters that the over-pressure would need to be ten times greater for the glass to shatter, which was not much comfort for the householder who rang the County architect to complain that his ceiling had just fallen in. The Ministry pronounced the rugby field test a resounding success and even the newspapers believed that the sinister "sonic bang was not all it was cracked up to be". Even the *Guardian*, never a friend of Concorde, laconically noted "The mild reaction to the Government's demonstration of sonic booms had done more than calm the fears of officials responsible for the public relations of supersonic transport."

The public relations ritual in the skies of Huntingdonshire expressed the Ministry's deep anxiety about the boom. Whenever the public had been subjected to the explosive sound of aircraft crashing the sound barrier, complaints had poured in from irate householders, usually claiming compensation for broken windows and cracked ceilings. Now that Concorde was taking shape in the hangars of Filton and Toulouse, government scientists had to establish the boom's degree of acceptance among the ordinary tax-paying public, who could never afford a Transatlantic seat, and yet were pouring millions into Concorde's development. It now depended as much on the reaction of office-workers, school teachers and maiden aunts as on the expense account tycoons flitting between London and New York.

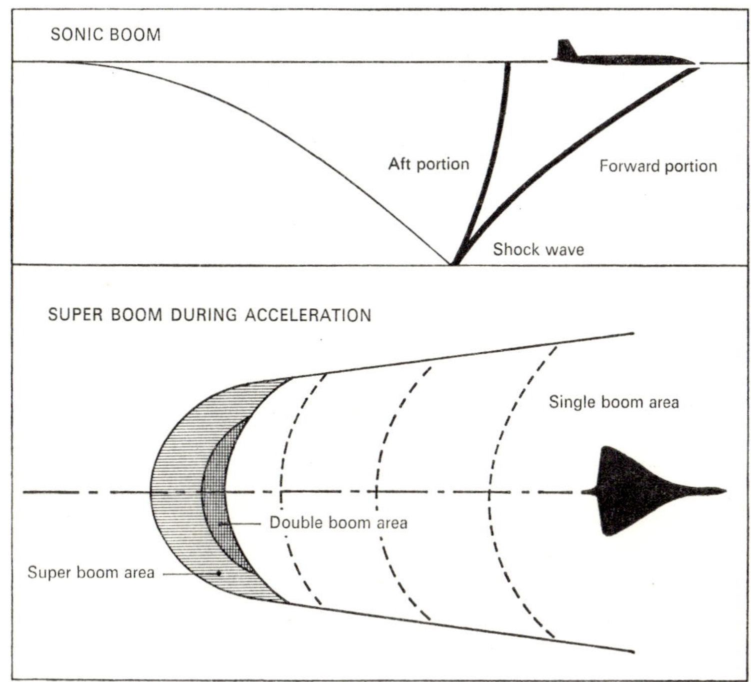

THE BOOM
(*Top*) Shockwaves caused by level supersonic flight.
(*Bottom*) Accelerating through the sound barrier the shockwaves overlap to produce superbooms.

It has always been the hope and intention of the aircraft constructors that they would be able to fly Concorde anywhere in the world, at supersonic speed. This is important to the aircraft's economics because the lucrative American internal market could account for many Concordes but would mean acceptance of the sonic boom over the American continent. Similarly, for European airlines, like Lufthansa, SAS and KLM to operate the SST effectively would mean permission to fly at supersonic speed across the British Isles. Sweeping a boom carpet across Britain, somewhat larger than a rugby pitch, each aircraft would trail a sonic bang fifty miles wide across the densely populated Midlands. The manufacturers shied off these problems in the early years, hoping they would go away. A joint declaration by Pierre Satre and Dr. Russell at the beginning of the Concorde project stated that nine miles up, "the calculated pressure rise . . . will in all normal conditions be less than that found to give rise to complaint. It may be that in unusual atmospheric conditions and with peculiar topography, a noise resembling thunder will be heard. But this will not be an inevitable and regular occurrence."

The Concorde's designers, however, for all their hopes of winning the battle of the boom, took the precaution of basing their market calculations on the most pessimistic assumption that the airliner would only be permitted to fly supersonically over the sea and "sparsely populated areas".

The boom, of course, is not a new phenomenon which has just erupted with Concorde. "Le bang sonique", as the French labelled it, was first heard on the day Captain Yeager crashed the Bell X-1 through the sound barrier over the Mojave Desert. It is a shock wave caused by the hurtling mass of an aircraft hitting undisturbed air particles in its path and cleaving a way through the atmosphere. Like the bow wave of a boat, it trails a cone of shock waves. The intensity of the shock wave depends on the speed and weight of the aircraft and its overall effect is unpredictable because atmospheric conditions can mute or intensify the pressure waves.

All the early experience of sonic booms came from relatively small fighter aircraft. In the United States, citizens disturbed by the sudden explosions were told by public relations men to accept them as the price of liberty. One Senator, incensed by unpatriotic complaints, warned the faint-hearted citizens "It is far better to listen to the sonic booms than to listen to the shrill, deathly screech of falling bombs." As the Pentagon ordered bigger and heavier military aircraft the bangs became worse, and the Public Relations department of Strategic Air Command distinguished itself by reaching new heights of rhetoric, "Many of the window-rattling booms which resemble the loud sound of a nearby thunderclap, are caused by the B58 bombers of Strategic Air Command—the only free world bomber capable of flying at twice the speed of sound." This was a new sales pitch that the makers of Concorde wisely rejected. Most people, of course, would perhaps be patriotic enough to suffer the occasional boom, but the dramatic, unpredictable thunderclap stirred up complaints and headlines. The most spectacular occurred on a humid, hot afternoon on August 5th, 1959, in the midst of dedication ceremonies at the new Ottawa air terminal. In the course of a military fly past, the pilot of an F104 Starfighter streaked in on a low level pass over the heads of the crowd. Five hundred feet up, with full afterburners blazing, he made a climbing turn, and broke the sound barrier in the transonic run itself, creating the most powerful of all sonic booms. The result was like an earthquake. The control tower literally exploded, showering glass everywhere. The roof of the terminal was torn open, the curtain walls were distorted and the exterior cladding crashed to the ground. Astonishingly no-one was injured, but the superboom of thirty-eight pounds per foot over-pressure, produced a damage bill of 300,000 dollars. In a dramatic demonstration it proved that a supersonic aircraft could rip buildings apart with a shockwave. Its potential as a war weapon did not go unnoticed by certain military observers. Such "superbooms" are the exception, the average boom being less than two pounds per foot, but even these can rattle windows and wake sleepers.

The American Defense Department, NASA, and the FAA were eager to find out how far American citizens would tolerate supersonic flight. They approached the problem in a characteristically direct way in 1961 with Operation Bongo over St. Louis, Missouri. The city, selected for "community response" tests was boomed day and night by B58 bombers, and loyally believed it was co-operating in national defence studies. There were few complaints until the mask fell and opinion pollsters revealed that the tests were for civil research. The citizens strongly disapproved of being treated like guinea pigs. If the booms were not for freedom, but to sell airliners, everybody would be far less co-operative with the authorities. This did not bode well for supersonic airliners. On March 5th, 1962, under the code name "Operation Heatrise", the U.S. Air Force tried once more to make the nation "love the sound of freedom". The thirty-two-ton B58 Hustler slammed across America from Los Angeles to New York at Mach 2 in just over two hours, the first plane ever to beat the sun across North America. At the Strategic Air Command H.Q. at Omaha, the most sophisticated radar net in the world was made redundant; in the words of one of the flight controllers "We knew where the Hustler was by following the complaints board!" The FAA, NASA and the Department of Defense pushed ahead with even more experiments. This time the lucky citizens "permitted to share in this patriotic undertaking" were those of Oklahoma City. On February 3rd, 1964, the second Operation Bongo began. In houses and office buildings throughout the city, engineers had wired up recording machines to find out how the buildings would react; scores of pollsters were on the streets ready to sample human reaction. Day after day at regular intervals the booms rolled over Oklahoma. In the first fourteen weeks one hundred and forty-seven windows were broken in the city's two tallest buildings. Opposition grew slowly after the initial jokes had worn off. Attempts mounted to get the tests called off. Federal judges heard an injunction and the Government wheeled in two psychiatrists to testify that outside stresses "such as the booms of the London Blitz" reduce suicide rates and admissions to mental hospitals, as a relief from "inner tensions". The injunctions were refused. One thousand, two hundred and fifty-three booms later it was all over. The results were inconclusive. Najeeb Halaby, who was steering a fragile American SST through its difficult infancy, told the London *Daily Mail* at the end of the tests: "As a result of these trials I am seriously worried about the effect of supersonic airliners shattering plate glass windows, or even damaging the structure of buildings. We have to face the fact that supersonic planes may have to be restricted to flights over the sea."

In Britain the Government was attacked as early as the summer of 1964 for ignoring the effect of the sonic boom. Concorde had few friends on the Opposition benches and the boom was an effective way of questioning the whole project. One Member expressed his concern that "Hundreds of thousands of people might be seriously inconvenienced for an increase in speed of travel of a mere few dozen!" This was good egalitarian socialist stuff, mixed with a criticism of advanced technology. The hardy Parliamentary Secretary to the Ministry of Aviation, Mr. Neil Marten, would have none of this feeble talk. He assured the House that a vast amount of research work had been done on the supersonic boom by his department, and that this was continuing. Perhaps he was remembering the time when he had been locked up in an open-topped box like a privy, at Aberporth in North Wales, and subjected to a battering by RAF Lightnings targetting on his ears. Anxious not to be influenced by the American tests he added,

"It is important that by this debate we should not generate any alarmist thoughts about the problem!"

He said that it was too premature to make any deductions from the American experiences, and that the British Government would wait for a full analysis before deciding whether or not to make "large-scale experiments in this country". Then with an ebullient confidence added,

"This is something people will learn to live with, just as they learned to live with railways, motorcars and jet aircraft."

Not everybody welcomed this manifestation of the second Industrial Revolution; *The Times* foresaw the world becoming noisier for millions, and acidly warned,

"The view of the Parliamentary Secretary to the Ministry of Aviation that 'people will learn to live with it' is complacent to a degree. Why should they?"

Why indeed. That was the question people were beginning to ask about the whole trend of modern technology and the industrial drive behind it. The Concorde was beginning to symbolise something more than the technical prowess of Europe and the United States. The prestige argument could well boomerang and show how antiquated were the concepts of de Gaulle and Macmillan at the inception of the scheme. In the minds of the Europeans, Concorde was comparable to the space programme in the U.S. with a similarly small return for such a mammoth outlay in resources. Technological wizardry, like patriotism, was not enough.

By 1966 the Government, smarting from its initial failure to kill the Concorde, was eager to seize any chance of escape. Any weakening of resolve on the part of the French Government or a technical set-back was certain to lead to a British demand for cancellation. Mr. Wilson's Cabinet hoped to be more fortunate than the Ancient Mariner; with the gentle peal of a sonic boom, the Albatross might fall from their necks.

The sonic boom offered an ideal opportunity for escape. If people living on Concorde's flight path were unable to tolerate its noise, then the British Government could proclaim the aircraft a technical failure. The only flaw in the argument was that a prototype Concorde would have to fly before the results of any tests could be conclusive. Until that time, only small Lightning jet fighters of the RAF were available for supersonic tests, no other aircraft of Concorde's size and weight existed for boom testing. If the Cabinet thought gloomily that the tests offered only a remote chance of escape from the Agreement, there was always the ever present chance that Concorde's ailment of constantly rising cost would be too much not only for the British Government, but even for the French.

In the spring of 1966, costs were clearly on the rise again. The House of Commons Committee of Public Accounts once again drew attention to the uncontrolled nature of Concorde's funding. They were particularly anxious about the way in which BAC was able to draw a profit from the development money. However much was invested, BAC took its normal profit margin for the work undertaken, but it was left to the company to decide how, when and where to spend the government's money. The confidence of the House of Commons in the way in which the aircraft industry spent the country's money had been severely shaken by the Bristol Ferranti revelations, unearthed by the tireless watchdogs of the Public Accounts Committee. Described by some as a public scandal and by others as a "mere accounting error" the two aerospace companies were instructed to refund a sum of over £8 million to Her Majesty's Treasury for overestimating on service contracts. It was discovered that Whitehall had paid twice for certain work and

Ferranti had made an 82% profit on missile work.

Unlike the Bristol Ferranti contract, Concorde was not a military project but the Committee were dissatisfied with the financial management of the colossal undertaking. They urged a "more detailed programme with the dates for different stages and the progress expected by specific dates; this, with agreed estimates, is considered to represent a joint Anglo-French development plan." As well as casting doubts on the way in which the contracts were being organised between the two countries, the Public Accounts Committee firmly said, "We note the Ministry's explanation of the considerable increase in the estimate of costs, but we doubt the value of estimates which are so conjectural as to be almost worthless as an indication of the ultimate cost." The House of Commons wondered how much the ultimate cost would be. Eighteen months after the last official estimates, Mr. Cranley Onslow, a Conservative backbencher, asked the Minister in the House of Commons on February 9th, 1966, to confirm that costs had now risen to the rumoured figure of £400 million. He reminded the Minister that the project was shortly due for a technical reassessment, and, alluding to the allegedly inefficient financial management, he told the House that "Many people in the aircraft industry considered that the cost control system of the Ministry was frequently time-wasting and sometimes downright niggling. That raised the problem of establishing effective Parliamentary control on spending." "Parliament", he went on to suggest, "should set up its own Select Committee for controlling the project" —the very idea gave hardened British aircraft executives a nightmare. They despaired that Parliament would ever understand the economics of advanced technology.

When the Anglo-French Concorde Directing Committee met in the last week of April 1966, it discarded all earlier estimates as "historic" and started to draw up new ones. Now they faced the requirement to finance two new prototypes to satisfy American airline demand for a larger production Concorde. The bill was expected to be almost double the existing estimate. Talks on Concorde were held at the highest level when the French Prime Minister visited London in July and informed sources in Paris suggested that even the General was becoming apprehensive about the escalating costs. This time Harold Wilson needed the General's help on other weightier matters, since Britain, once again, was to apply for Common Market membership. The French Prime Minister returned to Paris on July 9th and issued a joint communiqué that the British and French Governments were "confident in their intention of proceeding and that they were satisfied with the financial aspects." The two Governments finally steeled themselves to announce the new estimates on the opening day of the Farnborough Air Show. It was a massive £500 million.

On the day of the announcement the V.I.P. at Farnborough was none other than the Leader of Her Majesty's Opposition, Edward Heath. Quick to affirm his support for the Concorde project as a focus for Anglo-French collaboration, he argued "One could not expect to bring Britain back to the forefront of the world without being prepared to spend a lot of money." Just how much, he was later to find out. He told the bosses of the aircraft industry that the Concorde would provide a technological fall-out of benefit to all other industries.

Whatever the justification, trebling the costs was indeed a lot of money and Parliament was not slow to face up to its responsibilities. In a major House of Commons debate on November 28th, Labour Members called for the programme to be stopped. "The Concorde, at least in its early stages, was not for the ordinary man in the street. It would be for the international jet set, people playing the power game on other people's money, politicians, business men and diplomats", declared a Labour M.P. The Conservative Chairman of the Public Accounts Committee, Mr. Boyd Carpenter, confessed that none of his colleagues believed "that the figure would be necessarily as low as £500 million." He went on "It is an unsatisfactory state of affairs when the decisions of one Government to initiate and another to continue development of an aircraft are taken on figures which turn out to be so seriously underestimated." Niall MacDermot, the Financial Secretary to the Treasury, defending the Government, blamed the original Treaty. "The Concorde project is without parallel both in scale and complexity" he claimed. "The cost-plus financing of the contracts would", he told the House, "be replaced by an incentive contract system which the Ministry were evaluating." To many members this smacked of bolting the hangar door after the £500 million plane had got its wings.

Concern over costs was not confined to the English side of the Channel. The French may have been more concerned with prestige in the early days of the project, but the latest round of cost increases had frightened the Ministry of Finance. The "quartermasters" went to work and persuaded de Gaulle to sack the anglophile General Puget. He had given his word to control spending, but still the "lorry-loads of francs" were called for by Toulouse. It was enough for de Gaulle. After Christmas, Puget was informed that he was being replaced. Stunned, the ex-NATO air commander discovered his successor to be Maurice Papon, the outgoing Prefect of the Paris police. As France's most powerful Gendarme, Papon had been responsible for order in the capital, and knew more about the suppression of subversives than supersonic airliners. The prospect of the replacement of General Puget as President of Sud-Aviation by the ex-chief of the Paris Police met with less than wholehearted approval from the industry. A communiqué from the Sud-Aviation Staff Committee was published, complaining that General Puget had been given no notice of his dismissal, and darkly hinting that this might mean the end of "certain projects". The technocrats of Toulouse, who knew their previous master to be a champion of Concorde, did not find Maurice Papon such a sympathetic figure. His very first visit to the factory provoked a walkout. A joint works committee of January 2nd announced that the unions would take "all appropriate measures to get rid of him."

For a time, even BAC executives planned an intervention with an unprecedented personal appeal to the French Government. But nothing came of what would have been a spectacular banding together of international technologists to prevent what was believed to be political interference. The British press were full of rumours that the French had, at last, decided to drop the whole Concorde project, but in the cold light of Gaullist politics these turned out to be falsely optimistic. The Concorde was vital to de Gaulle's plans, but with a change of controller perhaps these plans could be achieved without the runaway costs that had upset the Ministry of Finance. General Puget was dispatched to Sweden as French Ambassador.

The new diplomat had scarcely reached Stockholm when the next threat to Concorde's life appeared. In the spring of 1967 the Concorde Directing Committee reached a serious impasse over the predictions of the airframe contractors. The problem was the proposed design for the production airplanes, which was due to be frozen into its final form before the end of April 1967. Circulating inside the Department of Economic Affairs was a crucial report on the economics and statistics of the Concorde's final version, made on the express orders of Mr. Wilson himself. Already the weight increase had been such that it looked as though the final production design would be more than five thousand pounds overweight. Some way had to be found of "sweating the excess off".

The design teams were confident that they could come up with a solution to lighten the aircraft, saving weight by re-designing an engine-bay here, a door frame there, or a lighter alloy on an internal bulkhead, thus gathering up valuable pounds. The civil servants on both sides of the Channel were sceptical, and said so. "It was a question of our word against theirs. The airframe contractors reckoned everything would sort itself out. We didn't, and we weren't prepared to argue" said one. The civil servants threatened that unless steps were taken immediately to bring the weight down, they would consider making recommendations to the Minister to abandon the project. The designers went back to their slide rules and eventually came up with a solution; a re-design of the entire rear end of the engines. To the British team it was a relief. They had always thought that the French petal-shaped nozzle was "the second most complicated orifice known to man". This was perhaps the most crucial re-design of Concorde. If the new nozzle did not work, the aircraft would cease to be a viable proposition for any operator; the heavier plane would either have to sacrifice its Atlantic range, or cut down on the number of passengers it could carry. Dr. Strang, Technical Director of the Filton Division, knew that it would be, "the aeroplane itself which kills the project". The pressure on his team was intense. "We had our moments but it was really a question of whether we could see the light at the end of the tunnel. Whether it was five feet or five inches wide."

The re-design worked and the Concorde Directing Committee heaved a sigh of relief although they realised that the development bill was bound to rise yet again. Responsibility for Concorde was taken over by the new Minister of Technology, Anthony Wedgwood Benn, in the autumn of 1967. He now assumed the unpalatable task of defending Concorde in a hostile Cabinet. A job not made easier by the fact that he was the Member for Bristol South East, the home of many of Filton's twenty thousand workers. It was unkindly pointed out to him that his constituency supporters were the most expensive Labour voters in Britain, and that it might well pay the Government to scrap the project and retire them all on full salary. It is not surprising that the Minister was reported to have confessed, "If only Concorde would crash on to Q.E.2, all my problems would be solved." Moving into his panelled office in Millbank Tower, high above the Thames, the Minister studied his files, and rapidly concluded that there was a large and dangerous gap between the assumptions of the planemakers and those of the public on the question of the sonic boom.

Until the summer of 1967, there were no intentions on the part of either the Government or the plane's makers to ban supersonic flying over land. In January the Concorde Sales Manager, Pat Burgess, had told a Press Conference that "BAC had studied a mass of evidence on public reactions to U.S. boom tests and feels that it will not be necessary to warrant a ban on overland flight." The airlines didn't believe that it would be banned either, for in April Sir Giles Guthrie of BOAC stated publicly that he didn't believe that "supersonic overflying would be restricted". Wedgwood Benn moved to open public discussion on the sonic boom. In his view, "It was quite wrong not to let people know what the sonic bang was like. There was at that time a great deal of ignorance about the sonic boom."

When the Minister first put forward his proposals for boom tests, they received a lukewarm reception from the civil servants, but in the words of one of Wedgwood Benn's colleagues, "when they were put to the Cabinet, they got overwhelming support". They felt that the reaction of public opinion would be so great that they would be able to back their moves for cancellation. Everybody waited eagerly to see what the results would be. It was perhaps only right that the first of the official tests took place over the city of Bristol where the Concorde was being built. To prevent bogus complaints, no warning was given, and when the Lightnings from nearby Boscombe Down thundered over the city there were only twenty-six complaints. On the five following days the number of complaints dwindled to six, but *The Times* letters page was full of debate from people campaigning for a complete ban, worried that "no part of our land will be safe from the cacophony of the Amsterdam to Acapulco, the Warsaw to Wichita and the Berlin to Boston flights". A Mr. Arthur Adams wrote to suggest, rather unkindly, that the acid test was to repeatedly boom the Prime Minister whilst at his holiday retreat. "Perhaps during August and September such a test could be carried out over the Scilly Isles." This was to prove unnecessary, since the Ministry decided as a *coup de grâce* to try out the boom over London itself.

The first flight over the capital by the Lightning succeeded in jamming the Ministry's switchboard—hardly surprising as it later turned out that there was only one line with three extensions available at the Concorde department in St. Giles Court. But it was the journalists who enjoyed themselves with stories of men who "almost fell off ladders" and shopping housewives who just heard a faint "pop". One man congratulated the Government, he was seventy-three-year-old pensioner Mr. David Jones, who had been gradually getting deaf over thirteen years. He claimed that his hearing was restored by the Monday flight over London. Commented medical opinion: "It is just possible that shock waves from the boom freed small bones in the ear which sometimes stick together and cause deafness." Several correspondents pointed out that the odd bang was hardly a fair test of the public reaction to what might be a day and night phenomenon. It was left to Philip Ehrmann, aged eight, to wind up the whole debate.

"Dear Sir, While in the Park yesterday I heard a big boom and all the Pidgeons flu off in a terrible fright is it fair to the Poor birds?"

After just eleven sonic booms the Minister of State for Technology, Mr. John Stonehouse, was able to tell the press that he "was delighted with the way in which the public had responded to the invitation to give their reactions". Everything had been "bang on". There had been more than six thousand "comments" on the test series and one hundred complaints of damage, mainly broken or cracked windows. Four thousand pounds was paid out in compensation but the Minister of Technology, Anthony Wedgwood Benn, held the tests to be inconclusive and said that "no decision has been taken, at this stage, on what restrictions, if any, should be imposed on supersonic flight over land!"

The supersonic tests over Britain that summer had startled more than the pigeons in the park. The Wilson Cabinet may have been vaguely disappointed at the level of public reaction but the airlines and the planemakers were now thinking hard about the possibility of reduced markets as a result of a ban on supersonic flight over land. They were alarmed that Concorde might not break even in everyday airline operation if unable to fly supersonic over land; some of the big American carriers would be particularly hit if not allowed to carry passengers coast to coast faster than sound, and American market forecasts would have to be drastically revised.

In one way the tests produced the result some of the anti-Concorde politicians wanted; they shook out a formidable group of adversaries for the SST. Suddenly the argument over Concorde took on an entirely new political dimension, spreading out from the lobbies of Westminster and the committee rooms of Whitehall, into the dangerous arena of public debate. Bo Lundberg had set an eminent example, speaking out against the noise pollution of the environment in the *Observer*. He had protested about the SSTs at the Montreal Conference of 1961, and now tried to protect the Eskimos as much as the well-heeled inhabitants of London and New York, writing in the *Washington Post*,

"The suggestion that SSTs should fly over sparsely populated areas seems to me a ruthless proposition. If sonic booms are unbearable for people in the cities, they are equally unbearable for people in the country."

In Britain the lead was taken by a schoolteacher named Richard Wiggs. Already a local campaigner against the forces of bureaucracy in his part of Herefordshire, he was moved by the Lundberg articles to write to the *Observer*, offering to set up a citizens' group against the supersonic plane, to be called the "Anti-Concorde Project". Just as Britain was ahead of the United States in building a supersonic airliner, so Richard Wiggs founded his movement six months before Harvard physicist William Shurcliffe started his "Citizens' League against the Sonic Boom", which included a caucus of Ivy League academics. Astute Washington politicians like Senator Proxmire, soon realised the value of this movement in their campaign to stop the SST programme and cut Federal spending. The movements had a wider significance than aiding the campaigns of politicians; they expressed, perhaps for the first time since the Luddites, a need to examine the value and method of technological progress. The European and American SSTs, because they were such clear breakthroughs, were seen as the manifestation of technological arrogance, and people were prepared to take political action to challenge the Government's right to take these decisions on their behalf.

It was the sonic boom which triggered the debate. On July 25th, 1967, Sir George Edwards, speaking to the National Aero Club of Washington about the Concorde, told them he believed that the sonic boom would in fact "be acceptable over populated areas". A week after Sir George's optimistic forecast that people would learn to live with the boom, three French people died in a farmhouse, near Rennes, Brittany. A farmer, Monsieur Prosper Meunier, his wife and three neighbours were finishing lunch with coffee when just before two o'clock a sonic bang from a fighter shook the old house and brought down the massive ceiling beams on top of the table, burying them under eight tons of barley which had been stored in the granary above. The three deaths brought a wave of public indignation, which swept France. It was also revealed that officially eight other deaths had been ascribed to sonic booms over the past four years, most of them from heart attacks at the moment of shock.

The farmhouse was not the first building in France to suffer; old towers had collapsed, and the Vezelay Church in Brittany had had to be shored up after persistent military flights. The Principal Inspector of Ancient Monuments, Monsieur Parent, was anxious about damage to the stained glass of the ancient cathedrals of Strasbourg and Le Mans. The French Ministry of Defence had set up an inquiry to study "appropriate measures for coming to terms with the problem posed by the effects of the sonic boom" and M. Parent felt that France as co-constructor of the Concorde ought to take steps to control future overland flight. "France is not only the country of the Concorde; it is also that of Gothic stained glass windows, and also the country which, at the Western point of Europe, will be crossed by most of the commercial supersonic aircraft." He then went on—"The fact remains that we must, some time or other, stop exploiting in all circumstances, the crude availability of technology, and limit its use to those particular instances compatible with the real improvement in living and this must imply the safeguarding of the culture and man's life." This plea for the quality of the environment went almost unnoticed in

France, but in Britain and the United States a segment of articulate public opinion was beginning to question the whole philosophy of Concorde.

6

Roll out and Recriminations

IT COULD have been a garden party—except that the temperature was eight degrees below freezing, and a thin powdering of snow lay over Blagnac Airfield. Chic air hostesses from customer airlines were trying to keep cheerful in front of a thousand guests as an icy wind whipped over Toulouse from the low hills of Languedoc. Ministers, top civil servants, and journalists from both sides of the Channel gathered to watch Concorde's roll-out. The airframe was now complete; and the aircraft would be moved from one hangar to another for further work and the whole world would have a chance to see her. For the Republic of France and the Anglo-French teams building Concorde, December 11th, 1967 was a day to celebrate. Jean Chamant, France's Minister of Transport, spared none of the frills of Gaullist rhetoric; he spoke for over an hour, and his listeners felt as if they were being dragged through an Arctic survival course. When it came to Britain's turn, Anthony Wedgwood Benn, Minister of Technology, was mercifully short and to the point. With a typical piece of English understatement he said:

"Britain, like France, has a great stake in Concorde. Our years of co-operation have only been marred by one disagreement. Up till now, we have never been able to agree as to how Concorde should be spelt. I have decided to resolve this myself. From now on the British Concorde will also be spelt with an 'E'." It was a gesture calculated to delight the French and annoy the Whitehall civil servants who, for years, had insisted on omitting the final "E" on all British memoranda. "The letter 'E' symbolises many things", Wedgwood Benn continued. " 'E' stands for excellence, for England, for Europe and for the Entente Cordiale." As his words echoed over

the frozen concrete more than one Englishman was pleased to see the Minister scoring points off the French. There were so many tricolours that anybody could be forgiven for believing it was a solely French occasion; Britain was represented by one solitary Union Jack, clearly home-made. The Royal Air Force Band, flown over for the ceremony, thumped out a rousing "Marseillaise", but "God Save the Queen" played by the French was almost unrecognisable to British ears. The strange rendering was charitably attributed to the cold weather. After the National Anthems, the two Ministers walked across the tarmac and cut the symbolic red, white and blue tape. The long hangar doors slowly parted, and the slender white form of 001 was towed out across the apron like a moth emerging from a chrysalis. It was a moment of considerable emotion; after five years' argument, threat and solid labour, the tangible symbol of the Anglo-French agreement was there for the world to see. For the French it was Phoenix resurgent; for the British a visible return on capital. The enthusiastic Minister of Technology told his audience that the first flight was planned to take place in the coming year and he knew that Stage Two had actually started with the preliminary assembly of production planes. "It is no wonder that those most closely connected with the project", he said, "should be experiencing mounting excitement." The delegation from BAC hoped the Minister included himself in that statement.

The world wanted to see Concorde fly, and the two test pilots, André Turcat and Brian Trubshaw, were eyeing the aircraft eagerly, as the spectators drifted into the empty hangar to thaw out on hard liquor; but a few hundred feet away in a second-floor office, a hasty conference was taking place to determine whether the plane would ever leave the ground. In a subtle piece of diplomatic one-upmanship, John Stonehouse, Wedgwood Benn's second in command, succeeded in gathering up a surprised Jean Chamant for informal and urgent discussions. The British Government desperately needed to know whether there was any chink in the monolithic Gaullist support for the project. On Saturday, November 18th, after a colossal run on sterling, the British Government had devalued the pound. The costly strategy, begun after the 1964 election, had ended in failure, and many Ministers now hoped that devaluation would allow the Government to make a clean start with a massive review of economic policy. The new Chancellor, Roy Jenkins, promoted since his early days as Aviation Minister, had to find ways of cutting Government expenditure so that resources could be diverted to the export industries. It was a matter of life or death, and many "sacred cows" of the Labour Party were listed for examination as possible expenditure cuts. If items such as prescription charges, so close to the Party's soul, were to be scrutinised, Concorde certainly could not escape, and the strong financial pressures to kill the plane were reinforced by the reports of the Directing Committee which gave a pessimistic view of operational fuel reserves.

Stonehouse's mission was to find out how far the French Government were disturbed by these developments. It was not without some trepidation that he opened the discussion with Chamant and parried the hesitant fencing of his embarrassed opposite number. Frank discussion was not encouraged by the fact that one of the sides wondered whether the room had been bugged. To the British Minister's surprise, a sudden thaw took place. It transpired that the French were also very much concerned at the rapid escalation of costs and like the British, they too had the dilemma of choosing between expenditure on roads, hospitals and schools, or feeding the ever growing appetite of the project. Although Chamant was not specifically committed, the meeting paved the way for an agreement whereby both Governments established objectives for the remainder of the development and production programme. In the words of one British Minister, "We thought that if the objectives were not achieved it would give us the right to withdraw from the original Treaty. This would save us investing in the full development and production programme." When both parties emerged from the office it was clear to the waiting BAC and Sud executives that they could not rely on unquestioning French support in the future.

The British set out for home, the Ministerial team congratulating themselves on what they considered a real diplomatic coup, whilst Sir George Edwards, Managing Director of BAC, from his long experience of Government frailty in backing the aircraft industry, had good reason to feel vulnerable and lonely. A Concorde prototype now existed, something to show for all the taxpayers' millions, but putting the aircraft into production for the airlines would cost

La Gloire. *(Above)* Fanfare for 001. *Toulouse, December 12th, 1967.* *(Below)* First Flight: Turcat takes up 001. *Toulouse, March 3rd, 1969.*

Waiting for the Crunch. *(Above)* The wooden SST that never landed on Horse Guards Parade. *(Below)* Bang tests over London—waiting for the Lightning. *Ministry of Defence Roof, July 21st, 1967.*

far more money. This vast sum could only come from the British and French Governments with their volatile relationship. Sir George knew for certain that the BAC team were going to be working "with a loaded gun at their backs". In characteristic fashion, he warned the politicians against "losing their nerve".

Sir George's grand scheme for a supersonic airliner was protected to a certain extent by Harold Wilson's renewed efforts to enter the Common Market. In January 1967 the Prime Minister, accompanied by George Brown, the Foreign Secretary, had toured the capitals of Europe trying to "moor Britain" alongside the European Economic Community. In Paris, the British pair had been courteously received by the General who listened to a long speech by Harold Wilson, which stressed "the importance of technology in our approach". Wilson wrote later of the meeting: "Both of us attached the greatest importance to our bi-lateral collaboration, defence and civil." Concorde was a symbol of the industrial and political independence that both the General and the British Prime Minister were seeking; the chance of playing a bigger role than that of "merely waiting in the ante-rooms whilst the United States and Russia settled everything". De Gaulle noted that Britain's evolution corresponded to his wishes, but in the General's mind, England was still not yet ready to "moor alongside Europe".

A further meeting in June, in the splendour of Versailles, found the General still willing to discuss broad philosophic themes, but on specific technological matters like aircraft, he was evasive. The main talk was about the Anglo-French variable geometry fighter, which the British Government was anxious to continue, and France wanted to abandon in favour of its own design. It was an ironic turn-about from 1964 when the British Government had wanted to withdraw from Concorde. The British manufacturers were unhappy about the French attitude, believing they had gained valuable experience during the period of co-operation. If the French continued with their own variable geometry design it would be a set-back for Anglo-French collaboration but as Mr. Wilson said: "Unlike the Concorde it was regulated by an agreement from which either partner could withdraw." The General's reaction, when these questions were put to him touring the grounds of Versailles, recalls Harold Wilson, was "an expression full of meaning".

In spite of the cordiality of the meetings there could be no mistaking the General's indifference to Britain's renewed attempts to join the EEC. As long as the Brussels negotiations continued, Concorde could not be axed without upsetting the French. As late as November 1967, the influential American journal *Aviation Daily* was able to note—"So determined is Prime Minister Harold

Wilson to break into the Common Market on the back of Britain's technology, that Concorde could by now be regarded as a safe project, beyond the point of no return, and clear of the threat of the axe." BAC were not so certain, for they knew that the Chancellor had raised his axe, ready to cut everything from the F111 to the National Theatre. On New Year's Eve, 1967, the *Sunday Times* observed, "The general pall of doubt and uncertainty is by no means evenly spread. It hangs a good deal more thickly over the heads of some industries, companies and individuals than others, as Sir George Edwards of the British Aircraft Corporation, Sir Giles Guthrie of BOAC and other worried men of Britain's aircraft industry are no doubt aware." Even the Common Market case for Concorde began to fade as the British Prime Minister realised that talks were at a low ebb. "Too much effort was going into the delicate footwork", said Mr. Wilson, "when the dance hall proprietor had already made it clear that there was going to be no dance." If there was to be "no dance", why hang on to an increasingly expensive admission ticket? This view was increasingly pressed in Cabinet by Ministers who had to face the painful task of making massive cuts to consolidate the sacrifice of devaluation. But Harold Wilson was as keen to enter Europe as Harold Macmillan had been, but now it was going to be a waiting game.

The atmosphere for taking the decision was fomented by the recrimination which had broken out between the British and French manufacturers. The aircraft so triumphantly rolled out in December had no chance of making its first flight on time. Delays were piling up. On January 19th, France admitted failure in keeping the deadline. There had to be a scapegoat but Jean Chamant, the Minister, could not have chosen less wisely. From the list of several hundred contractors, the name he selected for opprobrium was Rolls-Royce. The Paris–Bristol telephone lines became almost as hot as the Olympus combustion chamber. It was seven hours before the Minister retracted his statement, this time blaming a long list of subcontractors in Rolls' place, which, by a remarkable coincidence, all turned out to be British. The list included Elliott-Automation, Dunlop, and, singled out for special condemnation, Boulton Paul, manufacturers of the power-control systems which operate the rudder and wing control surfaces.

The Boulton Paul affair became an interminable dispute between the British and French, which still rankles. Delays and problems are not unusual on newly designed aircraft, particularly one in which the technical advances are so great, and nearly a year before Chamant's sudden announcement the British manufacturers had warned Toulouse that any further problems with the supply of systems could lead to major delays in Concorde's test schedule. But for diplomatic reasons, and the need to stay well ahead of the Americans, the French stubbornly insisted on keeping to the agreed date for the first flight, rejecting any excuses for delay at this critical stage. They also wanted to prevent the British Government levering itself out of the project, by using technical failure as a way of breaking the Agreement. Any faults had to be laid firmly at Britain's door.

The Boulton Paul argument became the focus for a great deal of bitterness, revealing weaknesses in the Concorde subcontracting arrangements. Under the terms of the Treaty both sides were to be given an equal share of the work. In order to ensure a fair division, contracts were apportioned by the joint Concorde Directing Committee. The main contractors, BAC and Sud, had therefore to accept the tenders from a list of pre-selected sub-contractors, placing them in order of preference and finally submitting three to the joint Technical Committee. This committee of civil servants then evaluated the tenders and recommended a supplier. It was only natural that the need to divide the workload and use a particular aircraft factory for political reasons, meant that the final choice of supplier did not always correspond with the wishes of the design team. This was exactly the situation in the case of the special glass for the aircraft's windows. Originally British Pilkington purchased the rights to a new formula for toughened glass made by Corning Glass Corporation of America. Because of French insistence on equal division of work, the Concorde Directing Committee allocated the windows to France. The French Pilkington Company had to make a fresh purchase of the patent rights and start from scratch.

The power-control system became the prime example of the inefficiencies of building a political aeroplane. When the tenders had been invited for the controls, Boulton Paul, an old established British firm, produced a tender which vastly undercut the French offer of Dassault, builder of the highly successful Mirage fighter. When the list went for evaluation, Boulton Paul found itself the preferred choice of the British, but not the French. There were strong rumours that the French were sticking out for the more expensive Dassault estimate because no less a person than the General himself had promised the contract to Marcel Dassault, the head of the company. Before they finally capitulated, after more than a year of argument, the French argued with some justification that Dassault had more experience with the controls a supersonic plane demanded. The mechanisms that have to operate the moving surfaces at supersonic speeds, are located in the hottest spots and hydraulic oils and rubber seals have to withstand a constantly high temperature without failure.

The experience of the British system has since lent weight to the French case, although it must be realised that Boulton Paul got the contract one year late and had to cram three years' development work into a far shorter time. The schedule was not improved by Sud-Aviation's attitude when the power controls finally arrived at Toulouse; they insisted on stripping them down, but found this a good deal simpler than re-assembly. The whole consignment had to be sent back to England, whilst Concorde 001 waited forlornly at Toulouse without its essential equipment. Even worse for the French, the British prototype 002 had almost caught up with 001 and was rolled out before very much had happened to the Toulouse version. Gallic pride was not altogether unruffled when a senior BAC executive publicly announced at a Bristol press conference that the British 002 would be in the air before France's 001.

Difficulties over components like the power-control systems underline some of the problems of building the most complicated aircraft ever put together from production centres all over Britain, Europe and the United States. The flying prototypes, 001 and 002, receive intense interest from press and television, but very little is seen of the immense operation which has made the aircraft possible. Within the United Kingdom nearly all the BAC factories are involved—Weybridge, Preston and Filton. BAC is responsible for 40% of Concorde's airframe—the nose, engine nacelles, rear fuselage, tail-fin and rudder. In addition it is the main contractor for the electrical system, oxygen, fuel, engine instrumentation, air distribution and de-icing. Aerospatiale have a 60% share of airframe work which is mainly the centre fuselage and wings. It is also responsible for hydraulics, flying controls, navigation, radio and air-conditioning. Like BAC, the French company is building Concorde in a number of plants all over France—at Marignane near Marseilles, Bougenais, Nantes, St. Nazaire and Toulouse. Feeding into the BAC and Aerospatiale factories are hundreds of subcontractors in Europe and the United States, transporting thousands of pieces of Concorde by road, and air, before fitting them together with fine precision in the main assembly areas. This can exasperate the engineers. "It would have been difficult to contrive a more impractical way of building an aeroplane."

In the early days the assembly of Concorde was not without its problems since many European manufacturers were inexperienced in the highly sophisticated technology demanded for the aircraft. The production skills that existed in the United States were simply not available in Britain or France. "We knew the quality of technology in the States", says George Gedge, Production Director of BAC Filton, and in the early days "We used to go round companies and say to them 'You are twenty years behind the times, mate. When you have pulled your socks up we'll come and talk to you.' " As a result of this blunt treatment many pulled their socks up and a number of shotgun marriages were arranged. "We sure have been brutal. Yes, sir", says George Gedge with the manner of a Texas oil tycoon. The impetus given by BAC and Sud to British and French, and even European, technology is one of the considerable benefits to have accrued from the whole project. The proof is in the smaller percentage of American equipment in the production versions of the Concorde compared with the prototypes.

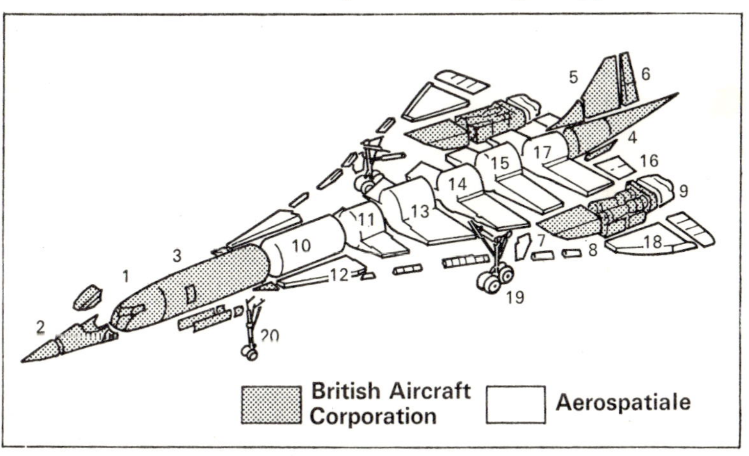

	COMPONENT	DESIGN	MANUFACTURE
1	Fuselage nose	BAC Filton	BAC Weybridge
2	Droop nose	Marshalls	Marshalls
3	Forward fuselage	BAC Filton	BAC Weybridge
4	Rear fuselage	BAC Weybridge	BAC Weybridge
5	Fin	BAC Weybridge	BAC Weybridge
6	Rudder	BAC Weybridge	BAC Filton
7	Air intake	BAC Filton	BAC Filton/Preston
8	Engine/Nacelle	R-R Bristol/BAC Filton	R-R Briston/BAC Filton
9	Nozzles	Snecma	Snecma
10	Intermediate fuselage	BAC Filton	Aerospatiale Marignane
11	Centre wing	Aerospatiale Toulouse & H. Dubois	Aerospatiale Marignane
12	Forward wing	Aerospatiale Suresnes	Aerospatiale Bouguenais
13	Centre wing	Aerospatiale Suresnes & La Courneuve	Aerospatiale Bouguenais
14	Centre wing	Aerospatiale Toulouse	Aerospatiale Toulouse
15	Centre wing	Aerospatiale Toulouse	Aerospatiale Toulouse
16	Elevons	Aerospatiale Suresnes	Aerospatiale Toulouse
17	Centre wing	Aerospatiale Toulouse & Fiat	Aerospatiale St Nazaire
18	Outer wing	Dassault	Aerospatiale
19	Main landing gear }	Messier-Hispano	Messier-Hispano
20	Nose landing gear }		

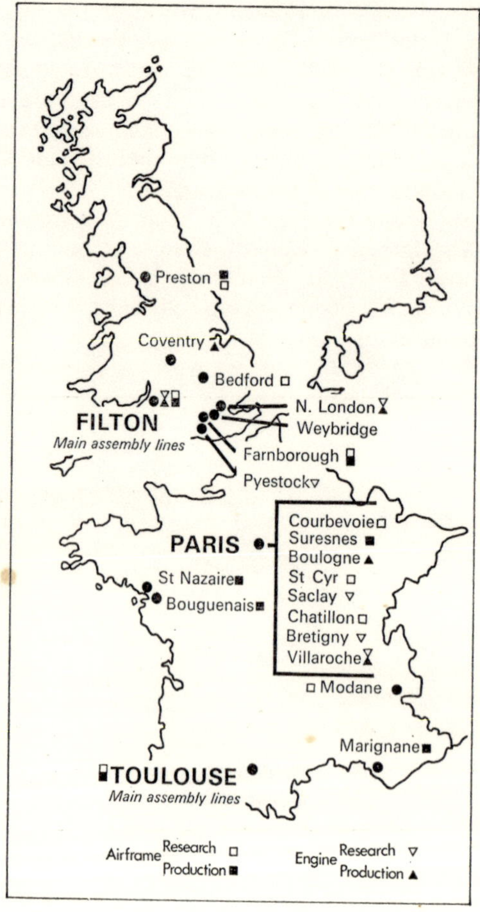

ANGLO-FRENCH MECCANO

The pressure to cut Concorde in the post-devaluation Spring of 1968 was enormous; but the aircraft miraculously survived. This time its defence did not depend entirely on the General. Even the French were becoming cautious about the project, as political and economic problems were growing thick and fast for the Fifth Republic. In Britain there was a different feeling. The country had endured such a difficult time with recurrent economic crises, devaluation and a drastic diminution of British prestige in the world; even the Labour Government which disliked Concorde hesitated at scrapping one British 'First', even if it was shared with France. One Cabinet Minister believed "We could not pull out East of Suez and cancel Concorde. It would be too anti-British."

The Minister of Technology, Anthony Wedgwood Benn, believed Concorde should prove itself. In his words—"Very few people realised that in that period, at about every six months, we went over everything—particularly the Concorde. But by this time it was becoming clear that the only sensible thing was to go forward and see where you were." Expanding on the case for saving the plane from the Chancellor's axe, the Minister felt, "It was not just that we had invested a lot and that it was going well. We did have an effective public revenue system where you had to fight like tigers for your projects, and concede many of them. But Concorde survived these tests not on the basis of emotional argument, but on the most elaborate calculations of money spent, investment to come, likely returns, likely sales and the costs of bringing in foreign currency. Another important argument was what damage do you do, if you appear to be somebody who can never follow anything through?"

The Minister had another reason for defending the SST. In the post-devaluation era, from his key position in technology, he was able to convince his colleagues that the aircraft symbolised the determination of Britain to export sophisticated industrial products, saving herself by her mental as much as her physical exertions. It was no good going back to producing cotton goods and bicycles, too many people could do that more cheaply in the latter half of the twentieth century. In Cabinet there were Ministers who took the view that such calculations were altogether too elaborate, and adopted what was later referred to as a "crude spending Minister's view". As Roy Jenkins, the Chancellor, insisted on expenditure cuts, the Ministers fought furiously in Cabinet, seeing the issue in the basic terms of either charging the public more for social services, or saving costs by a major surgical operation that could have an immediate effect—the scrapping of Concorde. Weighing all the factors, the Cabinet decided to exclude Concorde from the package of Spring cuts. To the acute embarrassment of the Labour Party, the Social Services Minister increased the charges on prescriptions, sacrificing an important principle of Socialist philosophy to keep alive what he, and many of his colleagues, regarded as a gigantic white elephant.

The anti-Concorde Ministers found one grain of comfort—the assumption that Concorde might kill itself. They hoped the airplane would fail the exacting tests it would have to pass before its airline customers became convinced of its viability. The agreement worked out by the British and French Ministers after the December roll-out had set a series of deadlines for performance, scheduled to begin in a matter of months.

"Fortunately for us the French sensibly took exactly the same view as we did . . . that nobody was going to build Concordes, mothball them and keep them on a shelf because people might want them later. On the other hand they did take the view", Wedgwood Benn observed, that "you should take it to the point of test to see if it met its specifications."

After the almost incredible escape from the Chancellor's axe in the Spring of 1968, Concorde seemed safe until she could prove herself in the air. Her chances of success were suddenly improved by events in the United States. The Anglo-French SSTs were in tangible metal form at Filton and Toulouse, when a crisis hit the American challenger, which was still little more than plywood and paper. To the astonishment of the aviation world, Boeing were unable to make their swing-wing concept work, after three years' research involving 4,000 engineers, and committing 25% of the huge corporation's resources. The swing-wing design which was meant to provide an aircraft which could cross the Atlantic at Mach 2.7 with 300 passengers, failed. In fact, after months of feverish activity in trying to reduce weight caused by the swing-wing hinge and its supporting hydraulics, the aircraft could not get across the Atlantic with a full fifty thousand pound payload. Boeing President, William Allen, asked the FAA for more time to secure "a sound foundation for an economically successful commercial aircraft". The design team asked for six months' grace to submit a re-design, which was granted by General Jewell C. Maxwell of the FAA. Boeings had tried to take a leap ahead in European style, and had over-reached themselves. In Pierre Satre's words, "All those people with all those computers and all those theories, pushed too far." It was back to the delta wing and a major re-design at Seattle, and significantly for Concorde, the earliest flight of an American prototype had slipped back two years, and was now planned for 1972.

The Russians had more success with their SST, and were preparing to fly the TU 144 first, but nobody outside Moscow knew this. The last Western group to see the Soviet challenger had been a British party of V.I.P.s, led by the Minister of State for Technology, Mr. John Stonehouse, in the autumn of 1967. A red carpet visit had been laid on at the famous Tupolev works outside Moscow. After Toulouse and Filton, the Minister was surprised to find the Russian factory relatively primitive by comparison. There was the same unmistakeable pterodactyl shape, and the Western observers could not escape the impression that the thickset workers, clambering all over the sophisticated airframe, were peasants straight from the steppes. The paradox was sharpened by the fact that the supersonic airliner was planned for the jet-set market that the Russians wanted to break into. Moved by the occasion, the British Minister seized

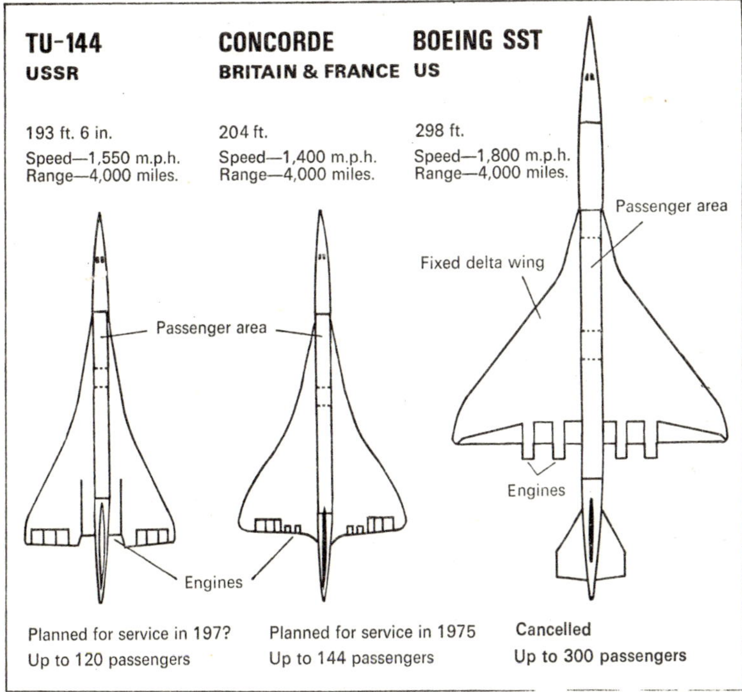

the opportunity for an impromptu address. Motioning to the workers, through an interpreter, John Stonehouse made a brief speech about international friendship and co-operation, in the shadow of the TU 144. The Russians broke into spontaneous cheers. It was an intriguing incident that brought together for a few moments, a British Cabinet Minister, moved by a sense of history, Russian workers, and twentieth century technology. Later when the Western press were trying to find out the details of his visit, Stonehouse was careful not to offend his hosts by revealing any secrets about the plane.

The TU 144 turned out to be very similar to Concorde in shape and size, but this did not surprise the British designers. There was much talk of the Soviets stealing a march by a highly organised spy-network that depended on East German cloak and dagger agents, vodka parties at the Soviet Embassy, and microfilm concealed in toothpaste on the Warsaw–Ostend Express, dramatised by the arrest of two agents in France in 1967. To the planemakers, however, it was not sinister if the aircraft looked alike. After all they were to fulfil the same mission and fly at the same speeds with roughly equivalent passenger loads. The TU 144 was dubbed "Concordski" by the Anglo-French team. The chief difference was in the less sophisticated wing section of the TU 144, and the grouping of its engines together under the fuselage. In the opinion of Dr. Russell, the Russians "generally like to follow, rather than lead", as evidenced by a number of their civil jet designs which are similar to Western aircraft. The Concorde is no exception to this pattern. When Tupolev Jnr. was on an exchange visit to the French plant at Toulouse, his trained eyes noticed a change in the Concorde. Immediately he pulled out a tiny tape measure disguised as a key ring, and before anyone realised, had measured one of the engine air-intakes. The Director of the French plant, Bernard Dufour, a genial man, was amazed—"He just pulled it out, reached up and claque, claque . . . I have measured your air intake . . . I find you have increased it by nearly eight per cent", he added with a knowing smile.

As the Russians were going ahead with "Concordski" in the Summer of 1968, its Anglo-French twin ran into unexpected delays. France, always the more stalwart partner in the project, suddenly treated herself to what de Gaulle called "Les délices d'anarchie". The rioting students of the Boulevarde St. Germain and Nanterre dramatically presented the General with a revolutionary situation as they were joined by workers in all sectors of French industry, striking against the regime. Sud-Aviation's complex of factories stopped work and Concorde waited untended, a slightly forlorn symbol of the old regime, until the Gaullist Government settled the trouble. By the early autumn the staff were back and the plant was working at full stretch to catch up on the schedule.

The French workers were not the only ones to have a disagreement with their government. In Britain the BAC management rolled out 002 unceremoniously without flags and fanfares. In doing so, with a sin of omission or commission, they forgot to invite Wedgwood Benn. The British newspapers quickly smelled a story and thought the Minister had been snubbed as a gesture of disapproval towards the Government for not being more enthusiastic in support of Concorde. The Minister was hurt by the decision; after all, he was M.P. for Bristol, as well as being responsible for defending the project in Cabinet with its thousands of jobs. Whether the Minister was invited to Filton or not, the most important factor in keeping work flowing through the Filton factory was for Concorde to fly and prove itself, a moment awaited by both Ministry and Parliament with fading patience.

On December 28th, 1968, the Russians suddenly flew their TU 144. Pictures were seen on all the world's television screens and the Concorde Directing Committee knew that it had to get one of its aircraft into the air quickly to restore credibility in the programme, and keep two cost-conscious Governments behind the scheme.

"Now remember lads, the taxying trials were a great success, so if all else fails she'll make a pretty good taxi."

7

A Life of its Own

EARLY MORNING mist shrouded Blagnac Airport on March 2nd, 1969. The pressmen who had arrived to report the headline story, Concorde's first flight, settled down to hours of interminable waiting. For two frustrating days the weather had capriciously delayed the big event, and now an east wind prevented the critical take-off along the north-south runway, equipped with a giant nylon tennis net to catch the £12 million insurance risk should anything go wrong in the last seconds before lift-off. As the top executives of BAC and Sud-Aviation waited for the weather to improve, they knew that every minor delay would be magnified by the press and television. It surprised everybody when, shortly after midday, word spread that André Turcat, Sud-Aviation's Test Pilot, was going for the take-off. Sceptics found it hard to believe. For months now Concorde had been roaring up and down the Toulouse runways at full power on taxiing trials to check brakes, controls and engines. Even as the Olympus turbojets burst into life, there were those who thought that the take-off attempt could well end up as another routine exercise pleasing the hundreds of spectators who arrived daily at the airport. It was not until the gleaming white shape, belching black smoke, was racing across the airfield, accelerating by the second and shadowed by the photographic reconnaissance jets, that everyone sensed that the spectacular climax of seven years' work was approaching. Quite suddenly, twenty seconds after rolling, the nosewheel rose from the ground and Concorde lifted into the air for the first time with a shattering roar. The spectators cheered against the crackling blast of the Olympus engines, blazing bright orange under full re-heat.

From the moment it left the earth for a brief twenty-seven-minute flight over the spring fields of southern France, with nose and undercarriage locked down for safety, Concorde achieved a spectacular metamorphosis. It acquired a life of its own, with a popular mystique which impressed even its long-standing critics.

As André Turcat brought 001 in to land after a triumphant flight, he was feeling out the characteristics of the new plane with its thin delta and droop snoot. The people of Toulouse looked up as the elegant new shape came in over their heads to touch down with a roar. After she had rolled to a halt, Henri Ziegler, President of Sud, and Sir George Edwards of BAC went forward with Brian Trubshaw to press their congratulations. It was a moving moment. They had protected their dream-plane against the tongues of critics and the knives of bureaucrats and had seen it fly. Now it would be that much harder to kill. Crossing the tarmac, the British team must have had some moments of regret that the "gloire" was not theirs.

For André Turcat it was a moment of exultation. He was the hero of France. The intellectual pilot with the face of a medieval knight and the cool manner of a savant, was a native son of Toulouse. Whilst he had flown France's most ambitious aircraft, some of the old Turcat cars built by the family firm were running the streets of the "ville rose". To the excited crowd gathered around him, Turcat said, "It flies pretty well. It was as perfect as we had expected." The press and television reaction was enormous—for the French it really was a "technical Austerlitz". The airlines were caught up in the publicity slipstream; full page advertisements had already been booked by Pan American to tell the world that "before long eight sleek Pan Am Concordes will be among the first to welcome you into the new age of flying."

France had shown her usual skill and panache in exploiting the publicity value of the striking new aircraft. There has always been a noticeable difference in attitude between Britain and France towards the project, since the first metal was cut. The long line of French firsts includes the first prototype, the first flight, first through Mach 1, and significantly, first to carry a Head of State and a group of journalists faster than Mach 2. It is hardly surprising that some people think the aircraft is completely French, and during de Gaulle's time, France appeared to be running the whole project. The Concorde mock-up at Orly Airport symbolises this proprietary interest. The life-sized model was once destined to be shown on London's Horse Guards Parade, but Sud-Aviation, in spite of previous agreements, failed to have it constructed in such a way that it could be easily dismantled, and shipped to England. When BAC officials hopefully looked it over they discovered that the only method of moving the wooden Concorde to England was by barge down the Seine, across the Channel, and up the Thames. Even if they had achieved this spectacular feat, the Ministry of Works stood ready to deny them access to Horse Guards Parade, which, according to regulations, cannot be used for "commercial purposes".

BAC looked forward to having their share of publicity and knew they were not far behind the French. The test team were confidently completing taxiing trials on 002 at Filton, ready for the day when it would fly and bring the whole project to the point when public approval could be rallied behind Concorde, persuading a doubtful government to persevere with the programme.

It was Brian Trubshaw's job to take 002 into the air on April 9th, 1969. The day started badly. Watching eagerly with the TV cameras were the British Minister of Technology, Wedgwood Benn, determined not to be left out of the show again, Sir George Edwards and Henri Ziegler, together with André Turcat. At the end of the runway at Filton that had been made for the ill-starred Brabazon, Trubshaw started the Olympus engines. The plane was to make a fast taxi-run and, if all went well, make the first flight. But there was a snag, the re-heat system which sprays fuel into the jet pipe to give added thrust, failed on No. 4 engine. The engine was shut down, and Trubshaw decided to try again. This time the re-heat ignited and the plane approached lift-off speed as it raced over the dip of Filton runway. The watching crowds held their breath as at 120 m.p.h. the nosewheel lifted from the tarmac. "It looks good", Trubshaw told co-pilot John Cochrane, and instead of braking, as he had on every other occasion, he gently eased the stick back and took Concorde 002 effortlessly into a summer sky, leaving the assembly hangars melting into the distance. As Trubshaw pointed 002 east and inland towards the R.A.F. airfield at Fairford, Gloucestershire, V.I.P.s dashed by helicopter across the fifty miles of open country in time to meet the new plane as she landed. Flying at 200 m.p.h. with the droop-snoot lowered, Concorde was in the air, over England. That, for Sir George Edwards, was a considerable achievement. "This sort of event is better to look back on than to look forward to." He told the press, "I do not know of any way in which you could have had this flight five weeks after the first one unless you had the resources of the two countries behind you. I hope my successors will sell hundreds of Concordes."

On its flight from Bristol, Concorde had passed over the ancient market town of Malmesbury where in 1065, after intense ornithological observation, a Saxon cleric strapped on home-made wings and leapt from the parapet of a church tower. The birdman sadly broke a leg, but survived the crash-landing to tell people how he had experienced the fifty foot flight to the ground. Nine hundred and four years later the first British supersonic airliner 002 was approaching the runway when it too had its problems; Trubshaw discovered that both radio altimeters had failed. The ex-R.A.F. bomber captain had been test flying for almost twenty-five years, and possessed more than enough judgment to bring the multi-million-pound prototype in to land safely. The failure of both altimeters on the first flight was nothing compared to problems he had coped with in testing all kinds of military and civil jets. "In a crisis", he had said, "one becomes quite cold-bloodedly involved in just trying to save people and the aeroplane." In the small control room of the Fairford Flight Test Centre, everyone held their breath in a moment of tension, before the wheels struck the runway with a screech and the drogue parachute flew out to brake the machine to a halt. Television cameras brought the scene to millions of viewers, unaware of the tense drama which had just ended behind the scenes. In a spectacular seizure of public attention, the BBC regular programmes were broken into to show the take-off. For the first time 002 had its own small share of the glamour surrounding 001. "It was wizard—a cool, calm, collected operation", was the typical gruff comment of Trubshaw to the press.

The watching Minister of Technology was quick to comment, suggesting that the dramatic flight had been handled "in such a relaxed British way—something like a British cricket match—but a lot of people, including myself, will sleep more soundly tonight than during the past few days." He had good reason to feel relieved since he had announced to his colleagues in the Cabinet, Parliament, BAC, Sud-Aviation, and the press: "Concorde is going to prove itself." The joint understanding hammered out with the French Government after the Toulouse roll-out had stipulated regular reviews of the project, matching targets with objectives; the flight test programme was to be the most important objective of all, and many members of the British Government expected

Concorde to fail the rigorous examination. "The thought was that there would be so much drag at supersonic speed that it would not be able to carry any passengers at all between Paris and New York", said one Minister. The hope was that the plane would prove itself a commercial flop. If this meant waiting for a few more months of flight testing, it would be worth it. One leading Cabinet critic, however, felt that Concorde was buying itself more time, "With every year that went by it became more difficult to cancel. The right moment never presented itself. Wedgwood Benn would always make the most elaborate cases for postponing the decision." The Minister of Technology believed it was important for the Government to keep its options open, although it was useless to maintain the programme under false pretences. In his view, "One of the of the arguments I got accepted by my colleagues was that while it went on we must work flat out for its success. It was no use doing it in a surly manner, spending £1 million a week, this would have been absurd." The teams in France and Britain made use of the time and settled down to the long task of proving the plane, knowing that the critics were waiting to pounce. From the BAC board room, running the difficult test programme in a "goldfish-bowl" was likely to provide plenty of opportunities for questioning their wisdom and efficiency. In an attempt to protect themselves from a hostile reception, the manufacturers issued an appeal for special consideration from the press. "There will be problems", they announced, "all capable of being dramatised, and all of them, the manufacturers are confident, capable of being overcome by the normal engineering processes." Unfortunately the normal engineering processes of the media did not obey scientific rules of technology. When it came down to it, critics would point out that it was public money funding the whole project, from the titanium bolts to the glossy brochures, and the taxpayer had a right to know how his investment was faring.

In 1969 the men building Concorde felt that they might win the battle after all. "It had certainly been pretty tiresome from time to time to think that Concorde was about to have its bloody neck cut, but now it was up to us to make our contribution and to get on with the job of making people eat their words", said one of the test pilots. It was in this atmosphere of grim determination to make the scheme succeed that the flight test crews got down to the long and arduous job of proving that Concorde would do what its designers claimed. It is the biggest single test programme ever undertaken for a commercial plane, tying up Europe's most experienced test pilots and engineering teams for over five years. Only after a flight programme of more than four thousand, three hundred hours, and satisfying the stringent requirements of the Air Registration Board's inspectors, will the first fare-paying passenger be permitted to step into a Concorde for a scheduled flight some time in 1974. As well as performing the regular flight routines that airline pilots can expect, the tests will push the planes to the limits of performance; near to dangerous situations, like stalling, engine surge and cut-out and subjecting the airframe to violent vibrations by firing explosive charges fixed on its surfaces. The new plane must prove itself controllable and stable under all conditions, carrying electronic passengers to prove it—racks of measuring equipment whose micro-circuit brains are fed with information from sensors and metering devices attached to every part of the airframe, checking stress, temperature and movement. After every flight, the millions of bits of recorded information are fed into computers at the Flight Test Centres of Toulouse and Fairford. As the engineers are quick to point out, it is only one stage less complicated than space flight itself.

As with space flight, the Anglo-French programme is supported by colossal ground facilities. Every step has been taken to estimate the performance of the aircraft in the conditions of actual flight. The highly sophisticated "wave" wing shape has only been evolved after thousands of hours' testing on hundreds of precision models, many costing more than £1,000 each. Some have been dropped from helicopters and others complete with working under-carriages and droop-noses tested in wind tunnels to simulate landings and take off. After intense research the safest and most efficient configuration of Concorde has been arrived at.

The heart of the SST is its engine, and the development of the Olympus 593 has involved a massive programme of research and testing, embracing the resources of both Rolls-Royce, who took over Bristol Siddeley, and the French company, Snecma. The engines, which started with a thrust of 20,000 lb. in 1962, have now been pushed to a thrust of 38,000 lb., for the production Concorde. Thousands of hours of static testing have been spent in the sound-proofed test beds at Patchway, near Bristol, and at Villaroche in France. At Pyestock in Hampshire the engine has been operated for hundreds of hours at sustained Mach 2 flight, giant heaters warming the air to 153 degrees Centigrade before blowers force it into the intake. New solutions have been found to the problems created by the need to fly safely at supersonic speed. Turbojet engines need to scoop in air at subsonic speeds and a highly sophisticated system of variable geometry flaps and valves has been devised to bounce the supersonic shock wave at the entrance of the air-intake to slow down the air flow for the engine's acceptance. In one of the more unusual tests frozen chickens have been fired into the engines,

Curtain Call for Britain. *(Above)* "Felicitations!" Turcat greets Trubshaw after 002's maiden flight. *Fairford, April 9th, 1969. (Below)* The Men and the Machine: pilots and ground crew of Concorde 002. *Flight Test Centre, Fairford.*

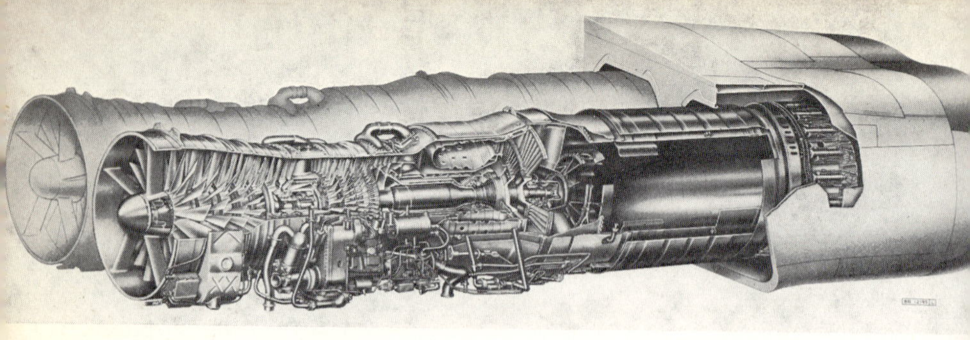

Power and Precision. *(Top)* Concorde's power-plant: the Rolls-Royce/SNECMA Olympus 593, 38,000lb thrust per engine. *(Above)* Carving Concorde's windows from solid aluminium with computerised machining, Filton. *(Right)* The man behind the Olympus: Pierre Young of Rolls-Royce.

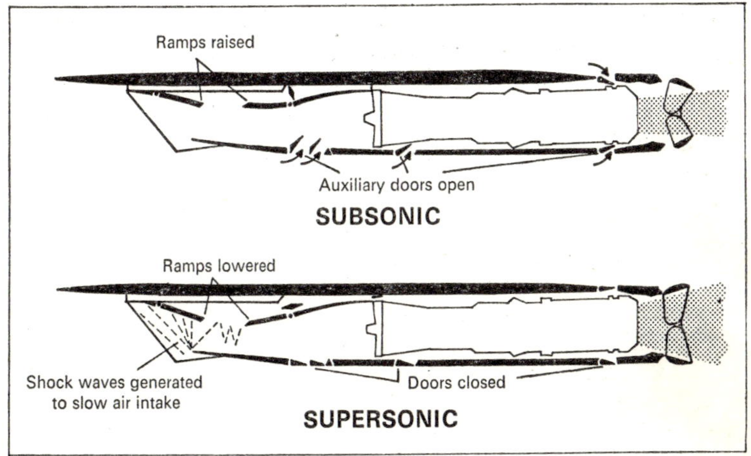

AIR INTAKES AT WORK

(*Top*) At subsonic speeds—computerised ramps and doors open to allow maximum airflow to the engine; exhaust nozzle in 'silencing position'.

(*Bottom*) At supersonic speed—computer adjusts intake configuration to create the shockwaves to slow the airflow to subsonic speeds. Nozzles wide open for efficient thrust.

running at full power, to simulate bird collision at take-off.

The enormous fuel requirements of the four Olympus engines called for a major engineering innovation. A multi-million pound 350-ton fuel test rig was built to simulate all the conditions of supersonic flight. This system is absolutely crucial to Concorde because not only does it have to supply fuel at up to 100 tons a minute to the engines on take-off, and balance the changes that occur in the transition to supersonic flight, but it also does the vital job of keeping the plane cool in the searing heat of Mach 2 flight. This full-scale model has enabled the designers to incorporate vital modifications that could otherwise have brought actual flight operations dangerously near to disaster.

The airframe has received the most massive and prolonged testing. After the Comet experience of structural failures, no mistakes can be afforded with Concorde. It was essential to test both the method of construction and the aluminium alloys being used to see how they would stand up to the rigours of supersonic flight. At the British Government test facilities at Farnborough, and the French equivalent at L'Hers, huge sections of Concorde were sealed in special containers and subjected to alternate cycles of heating and cooling by rows of infra-red heaters and liquid nitrogen. Row upon row of jerking machinery tested the actual metal alloys for fatigue and creep—subjecting them to the temperature differentials of flight conditions, and on a tiny island in the Atlantic off St. Nazaire, structural metal specimens have been lined up on the sea shore for corrosion tests.

In the most spectacular test of all a complete Concorde airframe has been encased in a huge metallic glove at Farnborough so that fifteen years of operational life, with cycles of heating and cooling, can be duplicated, with scientists checking every detail. After the aircraft has been in airline service for two years, it will be possible to predict, with absolute accuracy, how long a Concorde will last in the conditions of supersonic flight. The investment in the little seen or talked about ground test programme which has been running for over twelve years in the most advanced plants in Europe and which will continue for most of the project's life, is responsible for a major part of the final cost of development. The space programme scale of the operation has set a unique pattern for future international co-operation.

In the summer of 1969, with the flight test programme just beginning, the end results of all this time and effort were two tangible airplanes, whose job was to justify the vast amount of research and development. Although the flight testing schedule was pressing and any delay would cost hundreds of thousands of pounds, both governments felt it was time to show the taxpayers what they were getting for their money. The decision was taken to fly both prototypes at the Paris Air Show that June. It was a calculated risk. "Frankly if 001 and 002 collided over the Paris Air Show due to weather or both pilots having a heart attack", confessed Wedgwood Benn, who had to approve the idea, "the whole project would have been endangered."They made an impressive sight. George Gedge of BAC, Filton, who remembered Le Bourget, said "It turned my tummy over to see both of them flying at the air show." To another engineer it was like "hearing 'Rule Britannia', 'Land of Hope and Glory' and 'God Save the Queen', all rolled into one". The French, of course, naturally saw it as the General had always intended, as a symbol of *La Gloire Française*, but to the British team it looked like the beginning of a wave of popular enthusiasm for the project, which had never existed before. Optimism was in the air, and 1969 promised to be the brightest year for Concorde since the brash days of 1962, as BAC turned on a rare public relations performance for the British taxpayer that summer. At one o'clock on Saturday, June 12th, 1969, Brian Trubshaw brought the slender delta slowly in over the River Thames. Leading the Queen's birthday fly-past in the position of honour, he flew low over

Buckingham Palace, where the Royal family gazed up at the Concorde which had spectacularly become the focus of attention for thousands of Londoners. Basking in the sudden warmth of public and press approval was an entirely new experience for BAC, and many wondered how long it would last.

In the favourable climate, the Minister took advantage of the general surge of enthusiasm to announce yet another increase in costs. In May, just before the double flight at the Paris Air Show, he told the House of Commons that the new estimates were for £730 million, of which some £330 million had already been spent. The jump of nearly 50% over the previous estimates of £500 million had been caused in large part by the British devaluation, inflation and the need for further design changes on the production aircraft, which included revised wing tips to increase range, a longer fuselage and the advanced new one-piece engine nozzles which were going to save a vital 5,000 lb. on the payload. The Minister and his civil servants had by now solved the difficult problem of how to finance production of Concorde. It was no good building a prototype without the facilities for production models, and to do this it was necessary to start laying down the basic assembly line, investing millions of pounds in machine tools and sophisticated jigs, and finding work to keep the plant going. However much the Government and BAC wished otherwise, the capital required, estimated at £150 million in Britain alone, would have to come from the Treasury. The City would not entertain such colossal sums on an uncertain venture like the Concorde—particularly with its record of government vacillation. Nor was the Government keen to start writing blank cheques for production facilities that might never be fully used. The Ministry of Technology and the Treasury were able to solve the dilemma by using the new Industrial Development Corporation's responsibility. In the Act setting up this public body, BAC was entitled to borrow up to £125 million of government money on which interest would be paid at commercial rates, with the Government carrying the risk, and the Company could borrow a further £25 million from the commercial banks with the Treasury as guarantor. It looked a neat solution, and short of the nationalisation of BAC, which had been considered and rejected after deft manoeuvring with the City, it solved the immediate problems of finance, but it tied commercial decisions again to political considerations, which would bind Concorde still tighter to the vagaries of Westminster politics.

The 1969 test programme utilised both prototypes to gain the maximum amount of proving time, each flight by one aircraft was taken a stage further by the other. In this way it was planned to bring both to the crucial areas of Mach 2 as rapidly as possible. But delay hit the project. On August 7th, 1969, just six months after its first flight, the British prototype was grounded for modifications that included a set of more advanced 593 engines. It did not fly again until March 21st, 1970. Turcat, whose flight test programme continued during the British grounding, notched up another French first by taking 001 through the sound barrier on the first day of October, 1969. 002 followed almost six months later. Everything was running smoothly, and to raise political confidence the Minister of Technology was invited for a flight on April 10th. It was Election year in Britain, and the Government found it politic to show their confidence in the project, whatever the rumblings from the back benches. And so it was that a slightly apprehensive Minister waited in full flying gear for 002 to take off, posing for photographers. After a supersonic trip Wedgwood Benn was clearly impressed. "It is a marvellous aircraft", he told reporters. "It was a very quiet and a very smooth flight. I took off my wristwatch to hear the tick above the engine noise. What Rolls-Royce say about their cars certainly applies to their Olympus 593 engines."

The Minister's flight was the thirtieth of 002, and it was to be the last for another four months. This time an unfortunate series of union disputes afflicted the plane. In the run-up period to the General Election it was no small embarrassment for the Minister to find the expensive programme slowed down by a trade union ban on overtime; to many supporters of the programme it seemed almost treason. At least the manufacturers seized the opportunity to change the engines and modify the engine air intakes, ready for the next leg of the test programme. To many members of the Cabinet, Concorde seemed to be taking a very long time to prove itself, and patience was running out. Wedgwood Benn had warned the House in the Spring that there was an upper limit on Concorde spending, which was to be 15% above the £730 million announced the previous Autumn. If the ceiling of £830 million was exceeded, both patience and the money would be exhausted.

As the country went to the polls in the summer of 1970, pessimistic workers at the BAC Weybridge plant, who were already busy building production planes one to six, were taking bets that they would be on the scrap heap before September. The Labour Government was swept aside by Edward Heath, to the joy of BAC management who were confident that Concorde would now be safe, with the Conservatives back in office. Events were to prove otherwise.

The new government came into power with a tough, down-to-earth attitude towards British industry. There was an instinctive distrust of state help for "lame ducks", however distinguished they might be. The Department of Trade and Industry took over responsibility for aerospace and soon found its economic policy put to a severe test when the whole country was stunned by the news that Rolls-Royce was bankrupt. Mrs. Mary Wilson, the wife of the former Prime Minister, summed up everyone's feelings when she compared the collapse of Rolls-Royce to the loss of Gibraltar. The irony of the situation was heightened by the fact that Rolls still made the best engines in the world and had an order book many companies envied. However, the Company had been trapped on a hard contract in developing the RB 211 for Lockheed. It was the only British venture with the Americans and it was in trouble. Rolls could never recover the research and development costs on the engine from the contract sale price. The only way out was for the Government to take over Rolls, re-negotiate the deal and invest another £100 million in the RB 211.

The trouble at Rolls was serious for the Concorde project. The engine company was one of four main contractors named in the Anglo-French Agreement and if it suffered any dislocation, work on Concorde would be immediately affected. Also the French believed that any solution to Rolls' problems on the RB 211 would have an effect on the amount of money available for Concorde, at a time when decisions were needed on whether more aircraft should be built, to keep the huge production machine turning over.

The British Government had little choice. Rolls-Royce was rescued but the Cabinet must have reflected ruefully on the surrealistic economics of the aircraft industry. Even worse the plane-makers knew that they had made nonsense of the Cabinet's industrial policy, which would make it harder to raise money for Concorde or any other scheme. In contrast to the attitude of the previous Minister of Technology, the Cabinet refrained from giving any public approval or encouragement to the Anglo-French project.

For all the wavering support of the politicians Concorde has proved immensely popular with the ordinary public. At Fairford, 'Concorde-spotting' has become a sophisticated art, and the public car-park at the end of the runway deep in the Gloucestershire countryside is jammed by thousands of people who drive to see the aircraft fly at weekends. Fairford itself is a grey stone village on the edge of the rambling Cotswolds and seems about as far away from modern technology and supersonic airliners as it is possible to get, but it has taken a proprietary interest in the airplane, its crew and technicians. As Brian Trubshaw knows,

"Talking to people round here they are all surprisingly proud of this thing. Concorde's their airplane." A huge photograph of

Trubshaw's plane is pasted on the ceiling of the local inn, the Marlborough Arms, and shopkeepers have been quick to offer postcards and souvenirs. As one of them put it, "You can tell when Concorde is flying because the sales of plastic model kits rocket up!" The village also now contains an old English farm converted into a French restaurant.

It is not only in Fairford that the public crowd to see the aircraft. 650 miles away in France it is the same. The rooftop of the Toulouse terminal building is always crowded with eager spectators, and the bar downstairs is inevitably called Concorde. Although its plate glass doors have Caravelle-shaped handles, the bar changes its name, like a French street, to honour the latest national prestige product, which has the contemporary honour of having a pop-song "Zero Zero Un" dedicated to it.

The test programme moved steadily towards the goal of Mach 2 and full performance figures in a glare of publicity. Everything went surprisingly well—even better than the designers hoped for in their wildest dreams; figures thrown up by the computer showed Concorde to be within 1% of predicted performance estimates. There were still the disappointing set-backs. It was to be Trubshaw's personal moment of glory to bow Concorde into her top speed—a concession that Turcat and the French conceded after their long line of Firsts. On the appointed day in November 1970 when Concorde was to fly faster than 1,400 m.p.h., it was agreed that Trubshaw should "go" in the morning and Turcat repeat the performance in the afternoon. Trubshaw set out, only to turn back almost immediately because of a persistent red warning light. Turcat was already in the air waiting for news of 002. In Trubshaw's words, "To be fair to Turcat, he was prepared to hold 001, and I said don't do it." That afternoon Turcat announced over his radio that high over the Bay of Biscay Concorde 001 was showing her full paces. BAC had been pipped again. It was not until January 26th, 1971 that the British Concorde reached its full design speed over the Irish Sea.

Mach 2 is only one step in the four-year programme. A large number of unknown areas must be probed, from flying in the sub-stratosphere to flying in extremes of weather and temperature. All the time Concorde is having to be adapted to improve not only its commercial performance but also its public acceptability. Changes must be made to the engines to dampen the noise on take-off, specific airline requirements must be catered for. The Flight Test Centres at Fairford and Toulouse put the SST into the air as often as possible because the aircraft must still prove itself.

A typical test flight routine starts the day before flight, when the plane in its current state of modifications is cleared. With

Concorde there have not been as many faults as might have been expected with such a complex piece of new machinery. "Basically it is a very serviceable aircraft, the engines run like sewing machines." To a member of the Fairford team it is "remarkably good and the aircraft would fly each day if it weren't for the modification programme and component verification checks." On the day of flight the aircrew are briefed. Concorde is fuelled up inside its hangar and towed out to be connected to the ground systems generator, which supplies power and air-conditioning. The flight engineer is the first on board, about ninety minutes before take-off, for the long series of pre-flight checks. The pilot and co-pilot then join him, with the flight test engineers who monitor the banks of test equipment. After more checks the engines are started up, one at a time and tested, before the pilot requests permission for take-off. In the flight control centre the controller clears diversionary airfields around Britain, one by one, making a final check on the weather conditions and high altitude turbulence. Fire tenders take up their positions, and any birds sitting on the runway are dislodged by pistol shots. Concorde is taxied to the end of the runway for final checks and permission to take off. Then comes the moment when the roar of the Olympus engines reveals the colossal power at the pilot's fingertips. The brakes are released, and the crew feel a powerful surge forward as the plane starts to gather speed; at about 180 knots the nosewheel lifts off the ground and seconds later, with the speed just over 250 knots, the stick is eased back gently, as the aircraft roars off the ground in a steep climb, burning kerosene at one hundred gallons a minute.

On a typical test flight from Fairford, once the undercarriage is up and the droop-nose raised, Concorde 002 is headed east across the North Sea and clear of the busy airlanes that cut across England. At Mach 0.93, the streamlined visor is raised to prevent the windshield glass melting for the transition to supersonic flight. There is an eerie sense of quiet in the cockpit "The first time I locked the visor up in flight, it went so quiet I thought all the engines had stopped" was the reaction of Brian Trubshaw's deputy, John Cochrane. With reheats on and the engines up to maximum thrust, Concorde moves gently through the sound barrier. According to Brian Trubshaw—"Going through the so-called sound barrier is just a number on a clock, as far as this thing's concerned." Once the aircraft has passed Mach 1, on what the Fairford team call the "Round Britain route", Concorde banks to port and continues an accelerating climb north towards the tip of Scotland. As the speed moves steadily up, another set of automatic controls comes into operation. Fuel is pumped forward to adjust the centre of gravity and maintain level flight. Now moving at Mach 2, Concorde is flying smoothly as engines are throttled back to cruising speed. Another slight bank to port brings her round Cape Wrath, passing more than nine miles below. Now at 55,000 feet, Concorde is lined up for the straight seven-hundred-mile run down the west coast of Britain. The speed reaches twice that of sound, and, inches away from the crew's heads, the outside skin is hot enough to

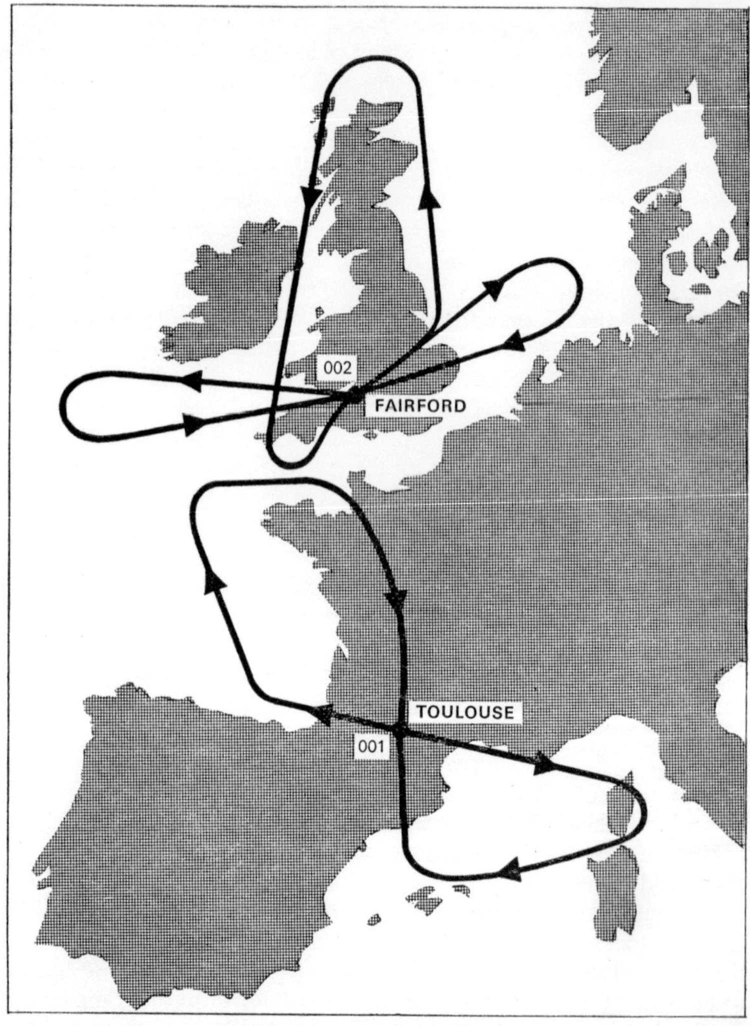

CONCORDE TEST ROUTES
Mach 2 down the back straight.

fry an egg. Sometimes clear-air turbulence is encountered when in Trubshaw's opinion "It rides rather like a fighter. I think you tend to regard the ride as much less likely to put you up in the roof, than in a slower plane." The main functions of the plane are now run by computers which keep the critical engine air intakes adjusted so that the supersonic air is slowed down to the right speed for the engines and the exhaust nozzles. Computers are programmed to take immediate action to compensate for a sudden deceleration and yaw, which might be caused by an engine failure.

The test crews begin to put the plane through its paces; deliberately pushing engine and airframe close to the edge of crisis. Stage by stage, and flight by flight, the pilot goes through a carefully organised pattern of test procedures, cutting an engine suddenly, firing small explosives attached to the fin to create jarring vibrations, or deliberately causing a flare-out in one engine to see if it can be re-started. If anything should go catastrophically wrong the crew must know how to escape through the explosively opened hatches. One such emergency did occur on the one hundred and twenty second flight of 001, high over the Bay of Biscay. Turcat was at the controls, approaching Mach 2 when one of the engines started vibrating. A flare-out, like a giant cough, had blown out the air-intake ramp and the leading edge de-icing equipment. Most of the bits plunged down towards the Atlantic, but some were ingested by the engine, running at full speed. Turcat shut down the engine immediately and brought the Concorde safely back to Toulouse. Other incidents have been surprisingly few and far between, given the crowded skies of Europe and the complexity of the new aircraft.

On the British test run, Concorde's 700-mile dash passes over the main Western Approaches to Europe with their stream of subsonic airliners flying over four miles below. After passing Cornwall, where the people below hear the sonic boom, the aircraft loses height and slows down. The balancing fuel is pumped from front to rear to compensate for the change in centre of gravity and the aircraft banks gently towards the South Coast and heads home for Fairford. On the runway approach with the nose lowered for visibility, the pilot has to pay attention to the unusual characteristics of delta wing since Concorde is flying on what is termed "the back of the drag curve". With undercarriage and nose lowered, the plane sweeps in to the glide slope some twenty-five knots faster than a conventional jet with engines under automatic throttle, and with fully automatic landing approach aids. The characteristically high pitch stays constant till at thirty-five feet it enters the ground effect (the cushion of air built up by the wings) then the nose pitches down quite strongly, controlled by the pilot till the main wheels touch the runway and the aeroplane "flares" itself and makes a graceful landing. As soon as possible the pilot and crew are de-briefed and the recorded results of the tests are analysed by computer. And so the pattern will be repeated till the end of the flight testing programme, expected in 1974.

The initial results from the first four phases of the flight test programme have been surprisingly good and have given Concorde some protection against critics who expected failure. Performance is in many cases closer than expected to specifications, and enough data have been amassed to give the airlines firm guarantees of performance of production aeroplanes. Serious problems would have seen the end of Concorde, which has now already proved itself. In the words of its Chief Test Pilot, Brian Trubshaw "Well frankly, I believe myself, and from what I know of the performance of the airplane and the studies we've done, I think it is an economic proposition."

Concorde had won the technical round in the battle, to the credit of its designers and engineers. But it was just one more round in the battle for the Anglo-French supersonic airliner.

"PERHAPS IF WE WIDENED THE WINGS, LENGTHENED THE TAIL, SHORTENED THE NOSE . . ."

8

A Case of Human Sacrifice

ON NOVEMBER 5TH, 1968, Richard Nixon was elected Thirty-Seventh President of the United States. As he was sworn in on Capitol Hill he inherited some of the most difficult problems any American President has had the misfortune to face—the troubled cities, the racial tensions, disaffected youth and the running sore of Vietnam. Many ordinary Americans could be forgiven for wondering whether the Republic would tear itself apart under the stresses of civil and racial tension. Technological virtuosity allied to fiercely acquisitive capitalism had made the United States the richest and most powerful country in the world, but if deep social and political divisions were the price for riches and power, many believed the price was too high. American technology was in the hands of large corporations who had a vested interest in maintaining the tempo of their business activity, without worrying too much about the political and social consequences. The Vietnam war symbolised this for many, since the interminable conflict seemed to add a great stimulus to the industrial-military complex. The Space Programme with its billions spent on hardware seemed another great indulgence, while millions starved on earth. Technology seemed to be a juggernaut out of control and Americans of all political persuasions were questioning this machine. There was one respectable cause which could unite them—the pollution of the environment. The physical as well as the social destruction of the American dream had emerged as a factor in the Presidential Election. Americans who would never dream of joining a demonstration on Vietnam, and who deplored extremes of all kinds, could make their feelings known about the spoliation of their continent. The SST, waggling its swing-wings like an enormous three-hundred-foot-long insect in Boeing's Seattle workshop, became the symbol of pollution, and united all those who were uneasy about America's progress. It was known that the President supported the construction of an American supersonic airliner, but political opinion would not automatically accept one, and the public's view would be crucial. The whole issue depended on Federal funding and each time the President sought a budgetary allocation the issue could be aired by those who hated the whole idea of supersonic transport.

As the President took office, doubt was clouding the SST issue on all sides. His task was not made easier by the astonishing failure of Boeing to reach specifications with the Dash-200 swing-wing design. The Company had outlined plans for yet another attempt at an SST a few weeks before Concorde's first flight. This undermined confidence in the programme, with people wondering whether more good money would follow the funds already spent. The Federal Government had nothing to show for three years' work and expenditure; it did not have even the politically advantageous position of the French and British governments who knew that the taxpayers were so far committed that it would be a waste of money to turn back.

The Boeing 2707, called the Dash 200 by its designers, had won the FAA competition in 1966, beating mighty Lockheed, for the most prized contract in commercial aviation. In selecting this famous company to consolidate America's grip on world civil aviation, the FAA had chosen carefully. Boeing's reputation as an aircraft constructor was very impressive, not only in the commercial field where it was supplying some of the most successful aircraft in the world, with the 707 and 727, but also in the military sector, where it had built most of the United States' bomber force since the Flying Fortress.

The Johnson Administration had appreciated that even the United States could afford only one type of supersonic airliner, and that the aircraft companies would be unable to find the one and a half billion dollars needed to finance the project. The design competition had been the only way acceptable to American capitalism of justifying the release of Federal funds. For the massive programme to be sold to Congress, it was essential that the new aircraft offered a healthy return on the taxpayers' investment and the FAA stipulated that the aircraft's efficiency should compare with that of subsonic airliners which returned 15% on capital invested. In setting out the specification the FAA remembered President Kennedy's dictum that the American aircraft had to be a *commercially* successful supersonic transport, superior to that being built in any other country of the world. It had to be bigger and faster than Concorde or the TU 144 with a speed of Mach 2.7, nearly half as fast again as its Anglo-French rival. Its passenger load on the North Atlantic was to be 300. This meant a formidable production aircraft with a weight of 675,000 lb. of which 58,000 lb. would be payload. Concorde's statistics were more modest at 385,000 lb. and 25,000 lb. payload. In meeting this specification, the designers had to deal with the same problems that confronted the British and French in 1961-62, but to an even greater degree. The airframe, which would have to carry twice Concorde's passenger load across the Atlantic carrying twice the fuel, demanded considerable aerodynamic innovation. Aluminium was ruled out as a material for construction, since it could not withstand the high temperatures of Mach 2.7. The engineers would have to use titanium and stainless steel, metals which were far more difficult and expensive to work than aluminium. Although unlikely to be daunted by the need for technological innovation, the American plane-makers realised that any breakthrough would have to be achieved within the restrictions of delivering a commercially viable product.

The Boeing Company had been working on supersonic flight since the 1950s when it had been an unsuccessful contender for the B-70 bomber contract. It was determined to establish itself in the market beyond Mach 2 and had set up teams working under T. A. Wilson, one of its famous engineers. The swing-wing design, which opened the door to Mach 2 for Boeing, was the brainchild of Holden W. Withington, and it had clinched the contract against Lockheed's Concorde-style delta. A plane that could fly efficiently at high speeds with swept wings, and yet take off and land with straight wings, seemed to be the perfect answer to many military and civil requirements. It looked deceptively simple, and Najeeb Halaby had incorporated the idea in the original FAA plan for the "Project Horizon" SST in 1960. Defense Secretary Macnamara set the fashion by ordering a swing-wing fighter, the TFX, for the American forces. Boeing leapt at the idea and having unsuccessfully tendered for the TFX, the representatives of the company lobbied hard for the SST, bandying the catchphrase around Washington "It don't mean a thing if it ain't got that swing." To a man of

Dr. Russell's instinct, however, it was courting disaster, "Anybody who thinks of a swing-wing is crazy, except for a specifically few military reasons. A swing-wing commercial plane is a bloody stupid idea. But the United States got over-confident—just like Rolls-Royce on the R.B.211—and like them, it took four years to discover they were wrong."

The swing wing had gone wrong almost immediately. The gigantic thirty-six-inch wing swivel required such complex hydraulic systems that it exacted a very high price in weight. Despite frantic attempts costing 22,000 hours on computers and 2,500,000 engineering man-hours, Boeing design teams could not sweat off the weight burden. Computer calculations showed Dash 200's weight to be 750,000 lb. when the FAA had stipulated a maximum of 675,000 lb. The aircraft would be enormous, and the money-making payload had disappeared. It would be unable to cross the Atlantic with its specified passenger load, and the sonic boom made by such a large aircraft would be louder than any other plane and almost certainly unacceptable to public opinion.

The Boeing swing-wing plane was fluttering to the ground when help came from an unexpected quarter. Jean-Jacques Servan-Schreiber, the French radical politician and editor of *L'Express*, put up a strong argument for the Boeing at the expense of his country's Concorde. In his book *Le Defi Americain* Concorde was dismissed as the last of an old breed, doomed by the titanium and steel plane with the swing wings. Servan-Schreiber claimed "On two essential points—use of an entirely new metal to crack the heat barrier and the swing wing to change speed . . . the superiority of conception is so dramatic that we have to ask why the Europeans never came to grips with it. We could have mastered both of these problems. It was a question of vision, planning, decision making and risk taking." He continued his polemic: "Contrary to what the British and French directors of the Concorde project may say, American superiority is not basically a question of dollars, but of industrial structure, far sighted vision and centralised control." However, their "vision" was just a little too far sighted. It turned out to be Satre and Russell who were right in their engineering judgement. The American technical and dollar base had induced Government and industry to over-stretch the state of the art. One of the Boeing men confessed "We never succeeded in integrating the design. That is, we could never fit the engines, the landing gear, and the wing pivots together and still make the weight requirements."

On December 8th, 1968, Boeing finally admitted that their flirtation with the swing wing was over. Plans were announced for a completely new design, a delta wing successor designated Model 2707-300, which had been dreamt up by an alternative design team. It was Boeing's third attempt, and Lockheeds, noting the similarity to their design, rejected several years before, felt very cheated. Across the Atlantic the Concorde's designers felt they had been vindicated as Boeing's considerable PR department did a quick volte-face. The Vice-President in charge of the SST told reporters that the new plane "was designed with the pilot in mind", admitting that the swing-wing plane on which they had worked for four years might have been "ultrasophisticated"; suggesting that some critics might have been correct in saying that it would have taken a "test pilot with a doctorate" to fly the Dash 200. In contrast, the new 1968 model was "designed to be flown by the everyday airline pilot". This admission marked a significant failure for American technology. The enormous advantages of the swing wing had been forgotten, and the yellow mock-up which squatted in its air-conditioned nest, gently waving its wings in time with the muzak, was hauled away and thrown on a select two-billion-dollar West Coast scrap-heap. By the time the decision to abandon the swing-wing concept had been taken, Boeing had already spent more than two hundred million dollars on research, eighty thousand hours on computers and eight million, five hundred thousand engineering man-hours on re-design. There was not one single piece of tangible airframe to show for the effort.

The SST headache became an urgent priority for the White House. The technical catastrophe at Boeings inevitably brought the Administration face to face with the sort of decision alien to Republican capitalist philosophy—to pour more dollars into a project that had run into serious difficulties, and which was creating its own public opposition in the vociferous "pollution lobby". Nixon, who during his campaign had pledged "to arm the people with the truth", immediately set up an *Ad Hoc* Committee to review the status of the SST programme. The Committee subjected the President's pledge of a truthful relationship with the public to a severe test. Drawing on detailed evidence from quarters as diverse as Najeeb Halaby, President of Pan American, and Dr. William Shurcliffe, the Director of the Citizens' League Against the Sonic Boom, the Committee delivered its findings to Nixon in March 1969.

The Report was a very different document to what the President expected. It was a potential bombshell to be de-fused as quickly as possible. The twelve-man team had taken the SST apart, above all raising serious doubts whether the plane would ever be commercially attractive enough to sell in sufficient numbers to repay the colossal Government investment. More significant was the doubt that the airlines could afford to buy the SSTs if they were purchasing new fleets of jumbo jets. At the time the 747 prototype was just appearing from the Boeing assembly lines. And however brilliant Boeing might be the Committee wondered whether the Company could make both the Jumbo and SST without overstretching its finances. As the Committee clearly discerned "The Government may be required to act as guarantor of, or to provide any additional funds needed by the airframe manufacturer." The sums were certainly staggering; Boeing's financial needs to make the SST, apart from the two prototypes, would be more than twice the Company's net worth. The consideration of employment which would have gained greater attention in Europe was dismissed by the Report, which stated that "employment should not be considered as a justification for proceeding with the program, but only as a dividend from it." Even on the expectedly favourable side of technological fallout from such a large investment the Committee concluded pessimistically "The SST program cannot be considered as providing unique technological in-puts to military programs".

The Committee had clearly struggled with the maze of problems surrounding supersonic flight. "Almost every economic aspect of the program reflects unverifiable matters of judgement with great variance in the opinion of the experts", reported the team. Then, pointing to the key problem, it said, "No doubt, all of the technological problems are eventually solvable, but how soon and at what cost? The record for new aircraft being designed to make technological jumps of this magnitude is confined strictly to military production. The record in those cases is not good. Production costs have often been more than three times what they were predicted to be."

The *Ad Hoc* Committee could not ignore the Concorde which had started the race in the first place and which was already flying. If the Anglo-French project were dropped, then it would be possible for the US to cast its own SST gracefully aside, but the chances of the US Administration succeeding in persuading France to drop the project, when the Prime Minister and Government of the United Kingdom had failed, seemed very remote to political realists. The Report, however, tried to be optimistic. "Cables from our embassies in London and Paris indicate that some British and French officials close to the program are sceptical of Concorde's commercial viability." And, if the Anglo-French Concorde refused to die quietly, with America out of the contest, there were other ways in which the European SST might be brought down. The Report suggested "US noise standards could conceivably bar Concorde from access to the principal US airports which would undoubtedly doom the Concorde program."

The *Ad Hoc* Committee's Report was critical enough, but the section on environmental pollution was positively damning. Noise was the number one target. The Committee recommended that SST flights should be restricted to operations over water because the "effects of the sonic boom are such as to be considered intolerable by a very high percentage of the people affected". And with the boom outlawed, airport noise would become a significant factor, likely to weigh heavily against the SSTs with their colossal engine power. As the *Ad Hoc* Committee pointed out "Aside from hearing loss, noise may cause cardiovascular, glandular, respiratory and neurologic changes." Noise, however, was just a quiet prologue to the rest of the section. This conjured up visions of turbulent flight that "could cause fractures in unrestrained persons", hinted at the toxicity of ozone, and warned of such excessive radiation that pregnant women in the first "trimester would not be allowed to travel in SSTs". The environment section concluded with dire warnings of the global impact of the water vapour injected into the upper atmosphere by a fleet of SSTs; hinting at catastrophic effects on the weather.

The Report landed on the President's desk in March 1969; mercifully it was confidential and not surprisingly Nixon decided to withhold it from public discussion for as long as possible. Its assumptions would clearly dictate the debate that could decide the fate of the American programme, challenging the validity of the economic arguments and giving official voice to the fears of the environmentalists. The Committee having turned down their thumbs on the American scheme hoped they could kill all SSTs if America withdrew from the race, since she was in a strategic position to down her competitors, with her grip on the world civil aviation industry. The possibility had to be considered that the biggest passenger market in the world would be denied to Concorde.

The President's immediate action was shrewd. He rapidly shifted responsibility for the SST programme to the Department of Transportation in April, whose job was to "advance the transportation art", embracing roads and railways. Not only would this prevent a conflict of interest with the FAA, but it would shelter the SST from Congressional sniping. A new Office of Supersonic Transport was set up headed by William M. Magruder—Mr. SST—an ex test pilot who had ironically headed Lockheed's abortive SST design team. It was to be his job to pilot the Boeing to success, and he was going to need as much nerve to weather the political turbulence of the environmentalists, as if he were flying a new prototype. It was a move which underlined the close link between the President and the SST that had continued since

Kennedy's inception of the project in 1963. As a special Congressional report was later to indicate "The involvement of Presidents Kennedy and Johnson in the SST program had been so deep that they, in effect, along with the various special advisory groups reporting to them, were practically running the program." Richard M. Nixon, like his predecessors, appeared to have taken the SST along with the White House as an almost customary trapping of the Presidency.

President Nixon did not release the *Ad Hoc* Committee's report to the public until October 31st following his request to the House Appropriations Committee for more money and a public statement of his intention to continue with the project. The Report shook Congress. There was fury on "the Hill". A key member of the Sub-Committee on Appropriations, Congressman Yates, was "amazed that President Nixon approved the request for the SST. The Committee, which consisted of many of the ablest people in his Administration, recommended overwhelmingly in favour of suspending work on the project." He went on to point out that the seven hundred and fifty million dollar limit promised by President Kennedy in 1963 had almost been reached and future estimates showed an overspending; he warned the President—"this is the logical time to call a halt to the program and I shall try to strike out the appropriation by my Committee." Nixon, however, had to ask for increased funds giving the anti-SST lobby a chance to attack. When his request for ninety-six million dollars reached the Senate in November, Senator William Proxmire swung into action. His main concern, apart from Federal funds being poured into a white elephant, was that commercial pressures would force the sonic boom upon people once the SST was flying. FAA chiefs conceded under the Senator's questioning that "pressures from the people who want to use this airplane for profit . . . may drag it into that market, which one might identify as east to west over populated areas." The President did nothing to allay the fear of a boom carpet across the US when he was seen telling a group of children on television that one day they would be able to travel from Los Angeles to New York in less than two hours; nobody was going to do that via the North Pole.

After tough in-fighting, a compromise was agreed with the anti-SST lobby, and a token cut of eleven million dollars was imposed on the President's request for funds, whilst the SST survived in the Senate and the House. It must have looked to Boeings, the pro-SST lobby, and the President that the remaining five hundred million dollars needed to put the 2707-300 into the air would come through safely. But they reckoned without the strength of public opinion which suspected the manipulators of the industrial-military complex at work behind the vast project. The anti-SST lobby girded itself for action, and found a vital ally in the press, which reacted in a hostile fashion to the vote. The *New York Times* wrote, "99% of the population who will never fly in an SST can expect sonic booms to shatter their peace" and warned that the "putative benefits of a hastily developed SST are so vague, the Administration and Congress have made an incredible choice . . . the nation will enter the next decade full speed ahead in the wrong direction."

The SST was fast becoming a symbol of the People versus the Administration. In 1970, the anti-SST campaign snowballed, stimulated by the large and politically respectable environmental movement. What had begun with Bo Lundberg's lone prophecies over a decade before, became an organised protest movement. The Citizens' League Against the Sonic Boom, started in 1967 by William Shurcliffe, a quietly spoken Harvard Professor of solid state physics, had become the focus of the campaign. Beginning as a group of nine members on March 9th, 1967, and working from home in Cambridge, Massachusetts, he started his campaign with a magazine advertisement paid for from an initial donation of two hundred dollars. He was honest. "From the start I and other members made it clear that I must stick very close to the most pedestrian truth; I was to indulge in no colourful writings; no rudeness, and I was to document all major statements." From the initial nine members the group grew to a membership of five thousand and achieved an income of twenty-five thousand dollars a year. With his sister and a few colleagues, the Professor mailed press, TV and radio throughout America with regular fact-sheets and bang-zone maps. They lobbied Congress and appeared on TV and before Congressional review committees. The tenacity and dedication of this small group out-manoeuvred Washington's highly paid aerospace lobby, one of the most powerful pressure groups in American politics. For a long time the aerospace professionals refused to take Shurcliffe's League seriously. But the politicians who were consistently opposed to Federal participation in the SST, discerned an important source of political support.

1970 was the crucial year for the American supersonic airliner. The Citizens' League Against the Sonic Boom played a key role. In the spring Shurcliffe published his "SST and Sonic Boom Handbook", selling for ninety-five cents with a shocking pink and black cover. Nearly ten thousand copies were distributed free to Congressmen, newspapers and the aircraft industry. Boeing executives and FAA officials found their copies concealed under plain wrappers. "I mailed them with plain brown wrappers, with no return address indicated, to reduce the chance that the mailroom clerk would collect and burn them." In March the various campaign groups delivered a second blow with a full page advertisement in the *New York Times* whose bold headlines told readers that the,

"SST AIRPLANE OF TOMORROW BREAKS WINDOWS, CRACKS WALLS, STAMPEDES CATTLE, AND WILL HASTEN THE END OF THE AMERICAN WILDERNESS."

Generations of urbanised Americans had survived on the subconscious belief that the great wild frontier of opportunity lay just beyond every city highway. The grim consequences of supersonic flight were listed under thirteen headings in highly charged prose with particular concentration on the sonic boom, whose "enormous vibrations" would disperse the Newfoundland fisheries, affect the nervous, endocrine and reproductive systems, and even damage unborn children. People were invited by the advertisement to believe that they were "locked in a small room, and the walls and ceiling are closing on us" and were warned that the SST typified "the sort of thinking that will lead our species into an unnecessarily short and miserable life." On one of six mailing slips at the top of the advertisement, readers were invited to mail the President opposing the SST on the grounds that, "Growth for the sake of growth is the ideology of the cancer cell."

The propaganda was highly effective and the average American might be forgiven for thinking that the SST was the metallic outrider of the Apocalypse, trailing in its awful wake not just the earth-shattering sonic boom, but widespread skin-cancer, and the fourth Ice Age. Nor was there any shortage of eminent scientists to support theories that the SST could trigger off one global catastrophe after another. None of these theories could or would be dismissed lightly by the Administration, and the Government's scientific agencies found themselves landed with the impossible task of allaying fears by having to prove the impossible. If a hypothesis had been propounded that the SST might radically upset the environment in some particular way, then, according to the critics, the implication was so serious that the supporters of the SST would have to prove *absolutely* beyond any scientific doubt whatsoever that this was not the case. This was clearly an impossible task with some of the wilder assumptions.

The environment debate rose to alarming proportions over the hypothetical damage that the supersonic airliner might inflict on the planet, but the undeniable damage being caused by industrial pollutants and motor-car exhausts were strangely relegated to the background. Vehicle plants in Detroit continued to turn out thousands of motor cars a week, which burnt millions of gallons of gasolene to produce the greatest pollution problem any country had known in history. Although the pollution caused by the internal combustion engine was only too apparent, and scientifically documented; to tackle it was a bigger political task than hitting the troubled SST. The aircraft became the symbol of the evils of runaway technology, conveniently assisted by the fact that the immediate threat was from the foreign Concorde and TU 144.

The environmental case against the SST is admitted by many of its proponents to be based on the slenderest of evidence, but some of the charges are potentially very damaging. The case against the SST can be broadly divided in two—the micro-environmental issues dealing with the more immediate and measurable consequences for the environment, sonic boom, engine noise and immediate air pollution; and the larger geo-physical issues which are much more difficult to measure and assess, such as oxygen balance, toxic additives to the atmosphere, weather modifications owing to the effect of water vapour, and radiation hazards due to ozone layer depletion. These latter issues have caused the most controversy, the difficulty being that it is impossible to say that any given physical change has *absolutely* no effect. Almost every change in nature produces another change, however infinitesimal. Estimates can be made of probabilities of radical and dramatic change and as more knowledge is gained these estimates can be made more reliable. In assessing supersonic flight in the atmosphere it can be shown that specific effects are relatively trivial in comparison with the same effects from other sources, but it is impossible to be absolutely certain of every consequence, even though the probabilities indicate that the effects will be negligible. For example, it is patently ridiculous that a fleet of five hundred SSTs will deplete the world's oxygen supply, on the calculation that even if all the world's available fuel were burned at once, only 3% of the earth's oxygen would be consumed. The argument that the increase of carbon dioxide from SSTs would cause the earth to heat up like a giant greenhouse is also extremely unlikely since the role of carbon dioxide has been shown to be of minor significance in determining atmospheric temperature and the contribution from the SST would be a very small amount compared to the world's many million vehicles.

There is, however, much anxiety about the heavy air-traffic in the upper atmosphere with the fear that a world fleet of supersonic airliners would discharge so much water vapour that a number of harmful effects would follow, such as major changes in the world's weather, possibly culminating in another Ice Age. This seems extremely unlikely, when it is considered that the amount of vapour deposited in the upper atmosphere, even by an SST fleet, would be less than one five hundredth of the amount injected daily by tropical cumulonimbus clouds. Furthermore, research shows that the forces which control the cycling of water vapour in the stratosphere are vast. The stratosphere is relatively dry, not because it lacks exposure to water, but because natural mechanisms tend to unload excess capacity fast enough to stabilise water vapour at a very low level. The SST threat to the weather has been rejected by two of the leading American scientific bodies, the National Academy of Sciences Committee on Atmospheric Sciences, and the Office of Meteorological Research.

But arguments continue about the upper atmosphere, in particular the ozone layer. Ozone molecules consist of three atoms of oxygen in combination, as against two atoms which comprise oxygen at a lower level—ozone is found at maximum concentrations at about eighty thousand feet (well above SST flight paths). This layer acts as a vital shield, filtering out harmful ultra-violet rays. If this barrier were to be weakened by the chemical effects of SST pollutants it could be disastrous for life on earth. The ozone concentration over a given point on earth, however, varies more than 25% seasonally and more than 10% daily and, with this substantial variation, together with haze and dust filtering out ultra-violet rays, the ozone risk should be seen in perspective. Moreover, observations by the Massachusetts Institute of Technology have shown that the steady-state water concentration of the stratosphere has increased over the last five years by more than 50% and that this has produced no corresponding change in ozone density associated with the extra water vapour. By no means all the academic scientists accept their observations, and some believe there is a real risk of environmental harm from SST pollutants at high altitude. The distinguished Professor Harold Johnston, of the University of California, for example, formulated a theory that the nitrous oxide in SST exhausts would result in "simply catastrophic reductions of stratospheric ozone." His assumptions of SST exhausts output, coupled with a static mathematical model, led him to deduce the drastic depletion in ozone. His theory was that the protective ozone would be reduced by a half in less than a decade with an increase in ultraviolet radiation which would mean "that all animals in the world would be blinded if they lived out of doors in the daytime."

The reaction was predictable; seizing on this latest prophecy of doom, headlines appeared from Los Angeles to London that the SST "could fry the earth". Equally distinguished scientists soon pointed out that the assumptions on which the model was based were inaccurate, and the model itself assumed a statistically restricted picture of the upper atmosphere. One leading European weather expert thought, "In my opinion, the danger has probably been overplayed, but in that no scientist could give a categorical assurance that there would be no effect at all." One British peer was so exasperated by the refusal of the environmentalists to recognise progress that he asked the House of Lords to note that highly distinguished scientists were sometimes known to make the wrong conclusions. He pointed out that the eminent men of the Royal Society had been so alarmed by the steam engine in 1825 that they proposed, "It is dangerous for trains to exceed 30 miles an hour because the air will enter the compartment and the passengers will suffocate." One further fact puts the risk of supersonic flight into perspective. Military aircraft have been flying supersonically for over ten years with thousands of stratospheric missions by bombers and reconnaissance planes like the ubiquitous USAF SR 71. Although their flights are a closely guarded Pentagon secret, these planes, like the U2, have the capacity to undertake high level reconnaissance over unfriendly airspace at three times the speed of sound, defying the missile threat. If stratospheric flight is likely to create unique reactions then some indication must have become apparent from these flights—but so far no direct scientific observation has been published.

If titanic changes are unlikely to be caused by supersonic aircraft, the more familiar nuisance of noise is an obvious disadvantage of supersonic flight, but is far easier to measure and quantify. People have strongly demanded that engine noise should be reduced since the jet engine has become a twentieth century irritant. SST engines will always be relatively noisy, but, with improvements in technology, they will not be worse than current subsonic jets like the 707 and VC10. Large resources are being expensively applied to deal with the noise pollution problem.

Throughout 1970 the environmentalists were campaigning for an absolute limit of one hundred measured decibels of noise level at take off and landing in the vicinity of airports, producing practical problems for the airlines and planemakers, whose current engines make more than one hundred and ten decibels. There were powerful political and economic pressures behind the noise restriction lobby. The real estate surrounding existing airports becomes increasingly valuable for building if the noise is reduced, so that, particularly in the American State- and City-owned airports, decibels can be measured in thousands of dollars of development money. Also it is plainly economically disadvantageous if airports have to be built farther and farther away from city centres. In 1970 noise control became an important issue of State politics and no one was surprised

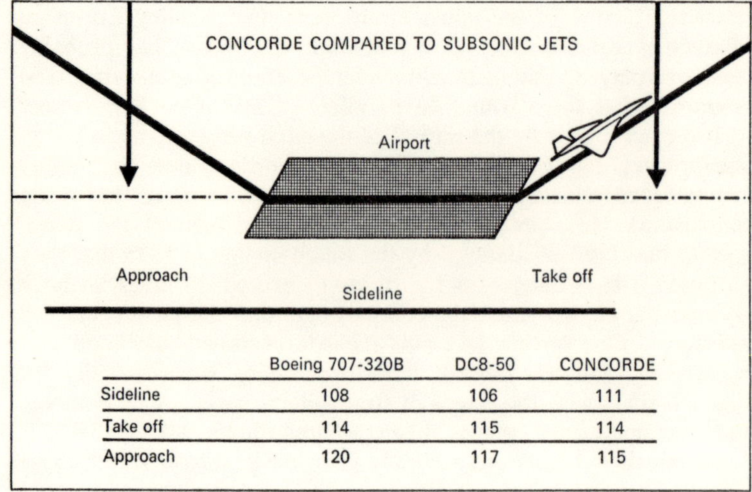

	Boeing 707-320B	DC8-50	CONCORDE
Sideline	108	106	111
Take off	114	115	114
Approach	120	117	115

CONCORDE'S NOISE RATING

As measured on the Epndb scale Concorde is level with most subsonic jets—but it has to come down to meet the 108 Epndb U.S. regulations.

when New York, with its airport problem, led the way. Once again the SST, which had not yet flown into an American airport, became the target for attack. Andrew Stein, Chairman of the New York Health Committee and an aspiring young politician, led the attack against the SST. In seeking to alleviate the sufferings of millions of New Yorkers whose life was made miserable by the increasing airport noise, he claimed: "These machines will make yet more noise and are not yet welcome in our states".

In face of the determined attack on the SST by the environmentalists, the plane-makers became alarmed. At Seattle three thousand six hundred skilled workers were already preparing the Dash 300 prototypes for construction. A giant mockup was being hastily assembled in an attempt to try and stem the rising tide of criticism. But like the Anglo-French project, as each month went by the cost began to rise inexorably. Some sub-contractors lost their nerve and decided to pull out of the project of their own accord, because of budgetary uncertainties and the mounting public campaign. If the SST was shot down, the Avco Corporation, Aerojet General Corporation and Tool Research did not want to plummet down with it. The politicians and anti-SST campaigners redoubled their efforts. The popular mood was turning against the SST and needed to be translated into votes which could effectively kill the project by cutting off its annual appropriation. To take on the Government, the anti-SST pressure groups allied themselves into a single confederation in the summer of 1970, which included the Sierra Club, Friends of the Earth and National Tax Action Inc. The new "Coalition Against the SST" organised itself to fight the President's request for two hundred and ninety million dollars needed to keep Boeing at work on the Dash 300. Marshalling all the paraphernalia of American lobbying, the Coalition aimed at sixty key senators. Inexplicably the resources of the aircraft industry and the FAA were impotent in resisting the challenge. On an NBC documentary, William Magruder was certainly flying in the wrong direction, blandly telling the nation, "The SST program is perhaps the only and certainly one of the few programs in which the taxpayers can invest their dollars and receive, as a partner in their investment, all of their money back plus one billion dollars in profit through royalties, and at the same time undergird our economy in America to the tune of better than twenty billion dollars over a twelve year period." Looking straight at the camera over the desktop model of the Boeing 2707-300 the ex-test pilot told them "Now this economy improvement is what's going to allow us in the United States to do these housing, education, transportation and environmental improvement programs that are so necessary. So the SST is good for Americans."

To most of his audience the SST was going to be positively harmful, the credibility gap yawned between planemakers and public. The anti-SST coalition concentrated on the one indisputable irritant connected with the new era of commercial aviation—the sonic boom. Whatever assurances the FAA, Magruder or even the President himself gave that the SST would not boom over America, the suspicion was deeply planted that once the SST ever got off the ground it would one day, in a sneaky way, boom all the way from Los Angeles to New York. It was a case of no money—no boom. The cards demanding an end to the SST filled the in-trays of Congress. The endless environmental row rolled on like a summer thunderstorm.

The Administration fought skilfully. On May 27th it persuaded the House of Representatives to vote in favour of the SST appropriation of two hundred and ninety million dollars, having wrapped up the SST's requirements in the total budget of the Department of Transportation. To halt the plane on a vote in the House would have brought the whole of Federal funding for roads, railways and airports in the United States to a standstill. The Senate, however, proved a different kettle of fish. In the late summer of 1970 a Senate subcommittee opened up a lengthy series of public hearings into the SST, airing every possible criticism. The ammunition in the *Ad Hoc* Report was particularly valuable. Witnesses were called from all over the world, including, from Britain, Mary Goldring of the *Economist*; some irate planemakers muttered that she should be sent to the Tower immediately on return. As the witnesses were called by the Chairman, who was none other than Senator Proxmire, the case against the SST programme was relentlessly pressed. The environmental arguments were starkly paraded and the economic arguments were torpedoed by a group of leading economists, headed by Professor Samuelson of MIT, who stated baldly: "Even if the SST had no adverse effects upon the environment in the forms of sonic booms and contamination of the atmosphere, it would be an economic and political disaster." Professor J. K. Galbraith of Harvard dismissed the balance of payments arguments as "strictly fraudulent and should detain no-one". "What is certain", he said, "is that the SST will cost a great deal of money that is needed for other things."

It was left to Najeeb Halaby to defend the dying SST, telling the Committee that the nation had to pay the price for staying in front. "Failure to support the supersonic transport program will ultimately mean that we run the risk of relinquishing world leadership in aviation as we already have in shipping. In view of what is already happening around the world in the production of steel and textiles and automobiles, there is compelling reason to hold fast to the production advantages we have in aeronautical technology." The whole anti-SST movement was not without its dangers he warned Senator Proxmire—"One of the terrifying things to one who is dependent on technology is that there seems to be abroad a feeling of anti-technology, technology is the devil that has caused every problem that we have in the United States today. But my only resource, the only resource for American industry in the future is to improve technology, without damaging the environment, so that we can meet the payrolls, can keep the ride going at a low price, can increase the size of the market." And if any of his hearers doubted his intentions to keep the ride going—at any cost—there were always the Russians to help. "That is the real threat we face, and, of course, if there is no Concorde, if there is no US supersonic, for which I think most of the world's airlines would wait, then the Tupolev is the only SST." On December 3rd, 1970, the Senate took their final vote on the appropriation after a three hour attack led by Senators Proxmire, Nelson and Muskie. The voting rejected the appropriation of two hundred and ninety million dollars by fifty-two votes to forty-one—a much larger majority against the bill than had been expected. The SST was almost dead.

Whilst the press and the Coalition Against the SST celebrated their notable triumph as the "victory of common sense over blind technology", the Administration fought back and tried to exploit the conflict between the House which had passed the appropriation and the Senate which had rejected it. To President Nixon the blow was almost a personal one, and at his news conference on December 10th, he told the nation: "What is involved here is not just the one hundred and fifty thousand jobs which will be lost if we don't build it, not just the fact that billions of dollars of foreign exchange will be lost if we do not build it; but what is lost here is the fact that the United States of America, which has been first in the world of commercial aviation from the time of the Wright brothers, decides not just to be second, but not even to show."

But the SST was not quite dead. Congress and Senate leaders reached an agreement to fund the Boeing project for a further ninety days until a newly elected Congress could make the final decision. It was purgatory for the men in Seattle who knew that their livelihoods were at stake.

The Administration prepared for the last round—but their opponents already scented a significant victory for democracy, achieved by a movement started by a small group of citizens. Where the "Peace Campaign" had failed the anti-SST campaign had begun to succeed. Moreover, if they were going to preserve America from the SST this meant making the whole world safe from the monsters.

There was a "special relationship" between the British and American anti-Concorde lobbies who watched keenly from the other side of the Atlantic as the American Coalition approached victory. Richard Wiggs, the leader of the British group, had also fought with advertisements calling the Anglo-French plane "a classic example of the Frankenstein syndrome; a monstrosity has been created which is beyond both the intentions and the control of its creators and which is revealed as an anti-social menace!" Unfortunately his great cannonade misfired because the British Prime Minister, Harold Wilson, chose the same day of the advertisement's appearance in *The Times* to announce a General Election. The French, of course, showed no sign of any anxiety about the environment, and were proudly flying 001 faster than sound over Metropolitan France.

With the Boeing 2707 almost extinct the Anglo-American environmentalists set about destroying the Concorde in New York at Stein's Health Committee hearings, which were held in a tiny room where the audience was deafened by the noise from a nearby building site. Richard Wiggs flew over to New York to present the case against Concorde, which was stoutly defended by the former Minister of

Technology. Wedgwood Been who arrived to give evidence. Wiggs immediately attacked the man who had once been responsible for Concorde—"Mr. Benn in fact only represents the builders of the Concorde and that section of the British Aircraft Corporation workers who seem to think they should be granted the privilege of continuing work on the manufacture of a machine which is both a prodigious financial loss-maker and an environmental monstrosity." When the ex-Minister's turn came he pleaded for a rational approach to noise control and told the hearings "Our progress towards man's control of machines must start with good decision-making and sound laws, just as it did for our forefathers when they mastered their harsh primitive environment and then later began to eliminate man's barbarity to man." Harsh words were exchanged when it was pointed out that the current problems were already on such a scale that the Stein Bill would force Kennedy Airport to close because none of the airplanes then flying would be able to meet its noise restrictions. "Man was not meant to live like an animal, cooped up", Mr. Benn was told. "He is supposed to open his windows and breathe some of God's fresh air and hear the crickets chirping", and the British team were curtly told by the *New Yorker* to "fly the supersonic monster between Britain and Australia so long as you don't bring it here."

It was not only New York State that started the campaign to ban the SST. The assumption now was that they were particularly noisy and particularly nasty; just as they were claimed to have a special capacity to destroy the environment. If the Boeing went down, there seemed no chance of Concorde being allowed to land anywhere in the United States. Everyone seemed to have forgotten the boom which caused the trouble in the first place.

It was only in England that the SST was regularly and officially booming living communities on the west coast test route, where Government scientists had wired cathedrals and buildings. In the early months of September in the ancient city of St. Davids in Wales, the Dean and monocled civic diagnataries nightly expressed their anxieties on television and to the press on the state of health of their ancient cathedral. Farmers complained that cows had aborted and hens stopped laying and schoolchildren with lilting Welsh accents told TV reporters how pets had jumped, and soup plates had been dropped in fright. There was a resentment that the "Men from the Ministry" in Whitehall were paying more attention to old buildings than to living people. The local feeling was and still is that the people in Pembroke have been used as guinea pigs in a test where human reactions to an actual environmental effect are the subject of less study than the Cathedrals.

While Concorde boomed down the west coast test route in the winter of 1971, in Washington the Senate was once more battling its way through Committee hearings on the SST. At the eleventh hour the aircraft lobby woke up to the challenge of the anti-SST Coalition, and started a massive, heavy-handed advertising campaign to stay in business. Bright all-American kids smiled out of newspapers all over the United States, holding aloft tiny models of the all-American SST. The reader was invited to speculate whether a true citizen would want his sons to see their inheritance snatched by foreign competitors, but the sales line on the SST not causing pollution made little impact on a public which believed that the SST meant skin cancer for millions. In the press and on Capitol Hill the counter attack raised the question of where the three hundred thousand dollars to sponsor such a campaign had come from when the aircraft industry was crawling for money. If the plane was such a good investment, why didn't the aircraft industry finance it themselves instead of asking for more money? The hastily recruited "Volunteers for the SST" were accused of being formed out of misappropriated public funds. The eagle-eyed Senator Proxmire uncovered a misappropriation of 12,892 dollars and 40 cents by the Department of Transportation in publishing and distributing a book of fairy tales about "a big friendly silver cat called Supersonic Pussycat who was all set to fly to Paris in two hours. But then along came a mean old Senator who cast an evil spell and so poor old Supersonic Pussy was never allowed to take off. Miaow, miaow, miaow! " The Department had to get out of the fairy tale business fast.

The slump in airline business associated with the huge red balance sheets of Pan American, TWA and others was thrown into the fight, and many doubts were expressed on Concorde's chances of success. Senator Reuss made great play of the fact that the French "wanted originally to cut the galleys" suggesting that "Perhaps they'll announce next that they would cut out the lavatories and thus operate on both ends of the alimentary canal at once." Even the much played up threat of the TU 144 and the fear of the flying hammer and sickle failed to rouse any more than indifferent support.

The SST's defence rested with Nixon, who threw his full personal weight behind the closing stages of the lobbying. Overwhelmed by their mailbags, the level of public debate, and by pressures from wives who were particularly attuned to the ecological issues, the Senators voted forty-nine to forty-seven against the SST funds. What many had seen as a flying dinosaur was finally dead, Senator Proxmire and the hardworking lobbyists of the Citizens' League

Against the Sonic Boom, led by Dr. William Shurcliffe, had succeeded in stopping American technology. Snubbed, President Nixon told the nation that the Congressional action "could be taken as a reversal of America's tradition of staying in the vanguard of technological advance".

The *Los Angeles Times* admitted that the aircraft "became the symbol of resistance to the so called military–industrial complex, a symbol of resistance to technological spoliation of the environment, even a symbol of distaste for President Nixon." *Time* magazine rationalised it as "A slowdown in the technology of haste", noting that "It was obvious to winners and losers alike that something new is afoot, a questioning of old values, old landmarks, old priorities."

The question in everyone's mind was would this mean the end of the Anglo-French effort? Now that the Americans had decided to opt out of the SST race would they force the others out too? The indications over noise were ominous. The British maintained a nervously respectful silence; the French, true to character, reacted differently. On March 25th, 1971, General Henri Ziegler, President of Aerospatiale, issued a statement. With French temerity he said that the future always disproved the beliefs of reactionaries. He pointed out that should the United States deny Concorde landing facilities there were other parts of the world like Europe, Asia, Australia, Africa and South America. The General ended his statement by declaring resolutely that "The Concorde programme must be pursued with more energy and confidence than ever."

9

Selling the Eight Hour World

THE TANNOYS directed the attention of the vast crowd towards the western sky and thousands of eyes strained to focus on an almost invisible shape, far away in the distant September clouds above Hampshire. Now and again trapped by sunlight the gleaming white delta materialised into the familiar Concorde shape. To the accompaniment of purple prose, Concorde's entrance was talked in over the 1970 Farnborough Air Show until the roaring of its mighty Olympus engines rudely drowned the loud-speaker. She flew gracefully over the hangars of the Royal Aircraft Establishment; rolling gently to display her fine form a few hundred feet from the line of Union Jacks and crowded terraces. Almost spontaneously, but no doubt encouraged by liberal hospitality, the thousands packing the tented chalets of the British aircraft industry rose and applauded the plane on which so much of their future depended. Even the normally reserved ranks of the press joined in the mutual celebration to the symbol of the future. As Concorde finally vanished into the westerly distance, the sense of occasion lingered on. The plane had stolen the show and given a vital fillip to her builders and indeed the whole of the British aircraft industry but *The Times* found, prophetically, "the British aerospace industry in a buoyant contemporary mood, but worried and uncertain over its future". Some observers went so far as to suggest that this would be the "swan song" for Britain's national aircraft industry. After all there were no new planes on show except the Concorde and the future appeared to hold little promise for the industry contributing £300 million a year to the balance of payments. The projected BAC 311 airbus was patiently waiting for £200 million of Government money and rumours were growing that Rolls-Royce was heading for the rocks. As the great hope of the industry vanished into the clouds toasted by the buoyant executives, at least everybody there believed that Concorde was living proof of the grand European design.

The Air Show saw Concorde still surviving the repeated attempts to kill it. Now it had somehow acquired a charmed life of its own; almost miraculously it seemed to the men who had lived through a decade of constant risk. The aircraft had weathered the storms of economic crises, the manoeuvring of politicians and a hammering from the environmentalists. Throughout the nine anxious years that Concorde fought for its life, it found little support from the world's airlines for whom it was being built. They had offered, at best, lukewarm support and played the usual routine of wanting something a little bigger, a little better and above all much cheaper. To this end they had noisily backed Boeing's jumbo-sized SST. Where Governments had said that Concorde would prove itself (with little faith that it would), the airlines were always coyly referring to the absence of "hard flight data", with the suggestion that it would not come up to specification.

The notion that Concorde would never attain its design performance was finally shattered by the figures coming out of the computers on the test flight programme in late 1970. They were little short of brilliant, surprising even the hardened designers at Toulouse and Bristol who had hit the target with errors of less than 1%. As Geoffrey Knight, Chairman of BAC Filton Division, put it, "On a project such as this any experienced chap knows that there is at least a 50/50 chance that the numbers will come out wrong. In Russia, the United States, Britain or France, on 50% of the occasions the numbers do come out wrong and I think it's fair to say we've had our moments of anxiety about it going under." Now the airlines for the first time would have to face Concorde as a fact of life, and with the British and French Governments hovering in the background like anxious mid-wives, the future of the plane became their responsibility. It was for them to decide whether they could make Concorde a commercial proposition; in this analysis it fell to the airlines to decide whether the project would survive.

The joint Anglo-French sales team which had been going round

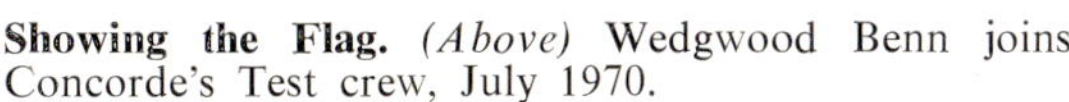

Showing the Flag. *(Above)* Wedgwood Benn joins Concorde's Test crew, July 1970.
(Right) Royal Approval: Birthday flypast for the Queen, July 14th, 1969.
(Below) Electronic passengers: installing twelve tons of test-gear in 001.

Supersonic Salesmanship. *(Above)* The fastest President in the World. Pompidou at Mach 2 with General Ziegler, Chief of Aerospatiale, 10 miles above the Bay of Biscay, May 7th, 1971. *(Below)* Waiting for orders. Concorde and Tu 144 at the Paris Air Show, May 31st, 1971.

the world for eight years were trying to convince potential customers that Concorde was a good thing for airline profits. Now the closer the aircraft approached its design performance, the more difficult it became to sell. Options had been taken out by sixteen airlines who represented 70% of the world's passenger traffic, and it was precisely these companies which remained less than convinced by the thousands of computerised calculations, statistical models and evaluations, which BAC presented to them. Stories leaked into the press seemed to indicate that the major airlines, including BOAC, found the operating economics of the Concorde-sized SST less and less attractive as the time approached to turn options into firm orders.

Pan American took the lead in "cooling" enthusiasm for the Concorde. The occasion they chose could hardly have been more appropriate, or the location more ironic. *Time* magazine sponsored a VIP study tour of the Concorde. Influential Congressmen, businessmen and top airline brass were flown across from the United States. At the sumptuous Air France building in Paris on February 7th, 1970, Henry Luce III of *Time* welcomed his guests to a magnificent lunch. Sparing no adjectives he extolled the virtues of the coming generations of supersonic aircraft which would improve international relations with "instant visits". "We are not bringing know-how or capital or artful salesmanship," he hastened to add, lest his airline guests wondered where his loyalties lay, "instead we are bringing affirmation, praise and perhaps an order book or two. The excitement of this visit is greatly heightened not just by the novelty of seeing Concorde itself, but by what it symbolises of the future and what it implies for the spectrum of that future which we trust will be broad and varied and brightly coloured."

The President of the world's most influential airline, Pan American, however, took it upon himself "to bring some cold oxygen into some of the euphoria". After a polite tribute to what he termed "this fabulous group of gallant Gauls and brave British" for an "unquestionable tour de force" he continued: "It is one of the most fabulous stories of forced technological growth in the history of technology and of man. The flight testing has gone unusually well and when four hard-bitten, well paid, clear eyed grizzled airline captains say it's well done, you know it is." It was only after he had carefully extolled the advantages for what he termed "the billion dollar show", as he liked to call the Boeing 747 (the description "Jumbo" was avoided for reasons of imagery) that Halaby began to turn on the "cold oxygen". He questioned whether the public might find Concorde "old fashioned because of its constriction, back to the tube, you might say, from the living room". He began to reveal doubts on other sensitive areas like operating costs, passenger capacity and maintenance expenses, all of which boiled down to a policy he described as "fly now, buy later". In a dramatic bid to avoid a decision he suggested that Concorde should be shelved and developed into a larger aeroplane, whose economics would meet new airline demands. The British and French plane-makers, still bearing the scars of their battle with the politicians and civil servants, winced when Halaby suggested, "For the long run, our brave British friends and our gallant Gallic partners and their Parliaments themselves have a very tough question. Are you prepared to produce a very limited quantity of Concorde 1, and then face up to planning and financing a Super-Concorde, an airplane which will better meet the requirements of both passengers and airlines, and will be superior to the Soviet and competitive with the US SST?"

The proposal astonished some of his listeners, who remembered that Halaby had been responsible for President Kennedy's SST back in 1963, and now headed the company which had rushed in first with Concorde options. He was now rejecting the almost completed plane, and asking for a Super-Concorde to compete with an American design which might never arrive. There was a sharp anti-British backhand at the end of his performance. "It is wonderful and remarkable to hear the Minister of Transport talk of Concorde as a vehicle towards entry into the Common Market and the suggestion by implication was into a United States of Europe; if that is so, then surely part of the cost of developing Concorde is Entente Cordiale, being now 'Entente Concordiale'. If he really means that, then surely the two governments can write off a very substantial portion of a two billion development cost as the entry fee into the Common Market." The brazen temerity of an American businessman telling Britain and France to scrap a project on which they had worked for nearly a decade and to write off the gigantic bill as the price of Britain's ticket to Europe must have come close to provoking a diplomatic incident. Afterwards, Geoffrey Knight, Chairman of BAC Filton Division, icily remarked, "I feel something warm and wet trickling down my back." "That was no knife", Halaby interrupted "That was a needle. And it was aimed lower than your back."

After *Time*'s Concorde jamboree, BAC and Aerospatiale wondered how serious Halaby had been in suggesting a larger plane, like the Boeing SST. The implied threat was clearly that Pan American might let its options slide, encouraging other American airlines to follow suit. The *Economist* naturally lost no time in calling for "the next British Government to get together with the French and talk seriously about whether they should concede some airlines' request to re-design Concorde". The manufacturers rejected this advice as totally unrealistic and did their utmost to express faith in Concorde's economic prospects, producing more calculations to show how Concorde could restore flagging business.

Concorde makes no sense at all unless it is capable of profitable operation and consequently some 200 sales to world airlines. Only then has it a chance of attaining the £4,000 million return to British and French balance of payments providing long-term production work for the European industries. The decision to build any supersonic airliner was based on the simple premise that the passengers would always demand faster travel, enabling the airline which offered a speed advantage to capture business from its competitors. In the early days the Concorde design teams were heavily influenced by the arrival of the first subsonic jets on the world's air routes. Pan American's decision to introduce the Boeing 707 on the North Atlantic in 1958 had given them an immediate advantage over their rivals, who had been rapidly forced to follow suit. Instead of droning across the ocean in a piston-engined airliner, the public immediately preferred the faster and more comfortable jets. Within two years no major carriers could fly piston and turbo-prop aircraft profitably on the North Atlantic route. The jets proved efficient, boosting airline profits, steadily lowering the cost of travel, and contributing to a staggering 15-20% growth in traffic throughout the 1960s.* There could hardly be a stronger argument for technological innovation creating efficiency.

The increase in business resulting from more efficient aircraft created work and viability for the manufacturers. Boeing received a substantial cash flow, and in Europe BAC with the 111, and Sud with the Caravelle, had a respectable portion of the market. The coming of the subsonic jets had been a dramatic and forced change; the airline chiefs could not forget that good piston-aircraft had been phased out well before the end of their serviceable life. Although the new airliners had increased their profits, they had also shown that the manufacturers could call the tune in the air transport industry by producing a pace-making aircraft.

This was exactly what the European plane-makers were planning to do. They saw that it was useless trying to compete with Boeing and Douglas on conventional jet airliners, where they would soon be out-produced and out-sold. Concorde itself, because it was advancing to a new state of the art, would obviously be more expensive than a 707 or DC-8, but the Anglo-French designers justified

* According to ICAO figures, by the 1970s 90% of the world's passenger traffic was being carried in 3,771 jets, and the remaining 10% travelled in 3,530 piston and turbo-prop aircraft.

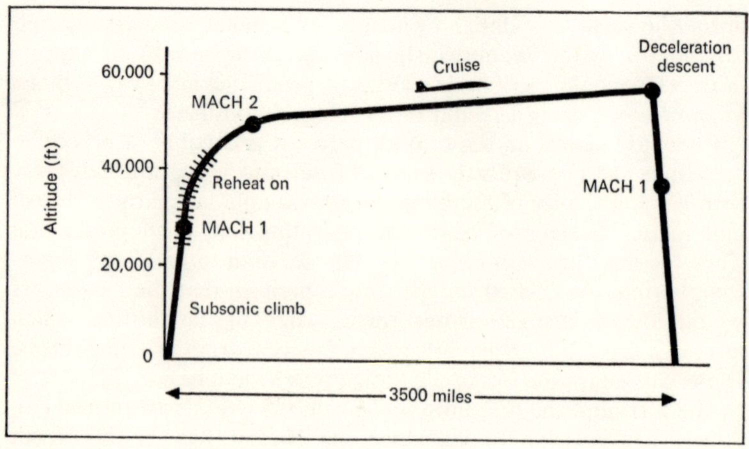

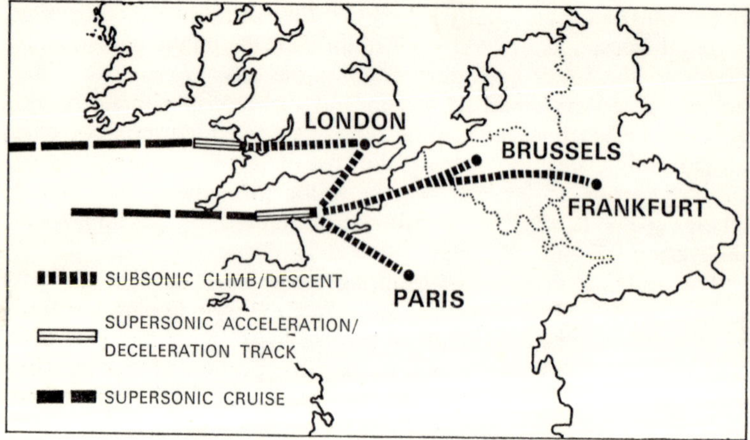

(*Top*) A North Atlantic Flight Plan.
(*Bottom*) The supersonic gateways to Europe.

the economics because the supersonic airliner's double speed would match the efficiency of conventional subsonics with increased productivity. A Concorde could make twice as many Atlantic crossings in a day as a 707, and so carry more passengers. In addition they believed that speed was highly marketable. However, all of this depended on when the airline market would be ready for the next technological leap and whether it could be persuaded that Concorde was the right aircraft for the job.

As early as 1961 market-analysis carried out independently in Britain and France for the BAC 198 and the Super-Caravelle led each country to believe that they could sell eighty aircraft of each type.

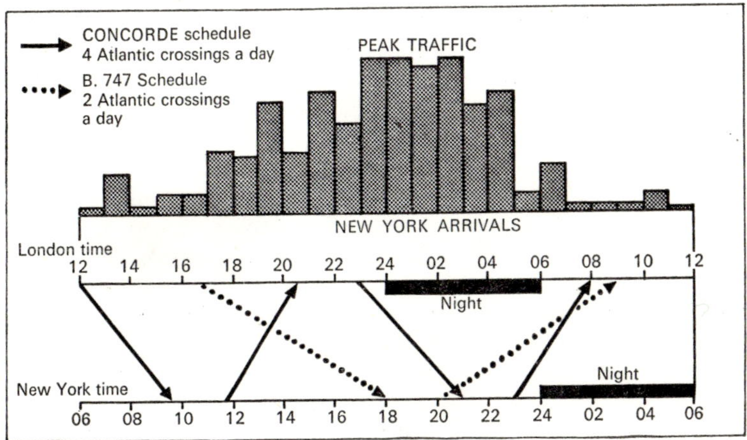

FOUR ATLANTIC TRIPS A DAY

Twice as fast as the 747 a Concorde service would revolutionise the schedules, and beat congestion.

These calculations were based on the then realistic assumption that the US supersonic airliner would arrive on the scene within three years of a European SST. The ability to sell eighty aircraft was an article of faith according to one BAC man: "the Cabinet made their decision to go ahead on the basis of around 160 aeroplanes". It was assumed that these sales would be achieved even if the sonic boom limited supersonic operation to flights over the sea. What the actual market would be by the time the SST was ready for service was little more than a sophisticated guess, dressed up as informed market research; even American methodology using some of the most powerful computers available could only reach an approximate answer.

A great deal depended on estimated traffic growth, which in the early sixties was optimistically put between 15 and 20% per year. To proceed with Concorde appeared to be both conservative and realistic, measured against American predictions that the world supersonic market might reach 500 aircraft by the 'eighties. Once the US had entered the race it was obvious to both the European and American planemakers that their own aircraft would be made to appeal to a different sector of the market. The sale of American planes depended on how large a slice of the market Concorde could win, which in turn depended on the time gap between the appearance of each aircraft. As Pat Burgess, ex-RAF bomber pilot and leader of the Anglo-French Concorde sales team, put it, "We said Concorde and the 2707 were compatible—not compatible in the sense that they would enter service in the same year, but with a five or six year gap between the two aeroplanes."

The thinking was that Concorde could switch to the lighter density routes once the Boeing 2707 became available for the heavy traffic. The airlines, of course, were prepared to play a hard commercial game to get the best aircraft at the most favourable cost—and when they were good and ready for it.

All the airline bosses knew, the first carrier to fly an SST would gain a huge publicity advantage and improve its passenger attraction. In the summer of 1963, Pan American had taken the plunge, committing itself to be the first airline outside the British and French flag carriers to place a firm option on Concorde. It was also a shrewdly calculated move to force the Kennedy Administration into backing an all-American SST, which was not only bigger and faster but which promised fatter profits. In taking options on six Concordes Pan American purchased a guarantee of being among the first in the field with a supersonic airliner, and ensuring that there would be two horses to back. The investment of around £100,000 per plane was well worth the risk. Options are relatively cheap compared to the actual cost of a plane. They are looked upon as a way of reserving a position on the production line, giving the airline time to think. The terms for taking options on Concorde are particularly favourable, since if BOAC and Air France fail for any reason to take up their own deliveries, the other option holders can withdraw without financial penalty. If, however, the aircraft meets its specifications, and Air France and BOAC take up their options (for which they have made no payment at all) then a foreign holder's money would be forfeit on withdrawal. Pan American's decision ensured that President Kennedy launched the American programme.

A curious race for options began even before the American aircraft was on the drawing board. By 1964 the FAA's office-bound assembly line had attracted forty-three options against Concorde's thirty-one. Many airlines which had pointedly said they were disinterested in Concorde, like Lufthansa, rushed for the US plane. The Bonn Government, anxious to cement Franco-German co-operation tried to persuade its national airline to be good Europeans and buy the Anglo-French plane. But the bosses of Lufthansa merely promised the concerned Bundestag politicians that, if they were forced to buy Concorde, it would sit firmly on the tarmac outside its hangar at Frankfurt. As the *Economist* pointed out: "The dilemma of the manufacturers and the governments backing them must be to know what weight to attach to any of these so-called orders. The financial penalty for not taking up an option is small. Airlines discuss it in terms of a booking fee, reserving the delivery of an aircraft that they may or may not want until they know precisely what it is and what they can do."

In the two years that followed, the Anglo-French manufacturers tried to increase the appeal of their aircraft with two major re-designs which substantially increased its payload and range. The proposed shorter range supersonic which was included in the Anglo-French Agreement to please France, died a natural death and sales targets were set at one hundred aircraft at an estimated price of £6 million per plane, against the original £3 million in 1962. Everyone knew this price, like all the others mentioned, to be inspired guesswork. The final magic figure would be a matter of agreement between the British and French Governments, who would need to levy at least £1 million per plane to recover the proposed research and development costs. But the reputation of the American plane-makers was such that the world's airlines believed far more strongly in the promises from Seattle. As one BOAC man knew, "Most of the world's airlines had bought American equipment. They hadn't been let down at that time. There was a feeling in the world that the Americans always made things work." The airlines were to be in for a rude shock with the failure of the vaunted Boeing swing-wing Dash 200, but in the early days Concorde trailed in the order book, and the critics seized on this poor performance as a way of ending the project.

In 1965, however, a sudden threat to the Anglo-French sales prospects appeared from Boeing, which was to prove more important for Concorde than the projected Boeing 2707 SST. In April the Company announced their intention of building a jumbo-sized successor to their famous 707. Frustrated by Lockheed in their attempt to capture the huge C5A military transport order for the Department of Defense, Boeing had decided to utilise this Pentagon funded airframe research and the Pratt and Whitney JT 9 D engine to launch a huge new airliner. This was a step forward in air transportation that was as significant as the supersonic. Juan Trippe, then Chairman of Pan American, liked the concept. American airlines were doing tremendous business in the middle 'sixties: the promise of an airliner carrying nearly 500 people over 6,000 miles gave prospects of dramatic cuts in operating costs. More important it would cope with the steady annual increase in traffic—assuming, of course, that expansion continued at a heartening rate. The cost per seat-mile, the yardstick of airline economics, would reach an all time low, and Trippe, seeing a chance of repeating early successes, ordered twenty-five jumbos from Boeing.

The rest of the industry could hardly stay out of the race. They realised, too, that passengers might prefer the larger aircraft, whose wide body broke away from the narrow tube of conventional jets. By 1967, 175 orders had been placed by US airlines and a further thirty-one by international companies, including BOAC. "At that point in time", says an experienced BAC executive, "they did not buy the 747 because they wanted to. They wanted to go on buying 707s and DC-8s that were turning in record profits. But they couldn't afford to take the chance that Pan Am had a saleable proposition which would leave them standing!" The Concorde sales team now had two threats from Boeing, which was awarded the American SST contract a year later. They had to start re-thinking their sales pitch. The 747 was selling an alternative way of dealing with growth. If airlines ruled out the speed factor they could make even more money as long as they attracted sufficient traffic to fill a good proportion of 747 seats. The other American plane-makers were not slow to follow the Boeing philosophy. Douglas and Lockheed soon put in hand their own "wide bodied" jets to carry large numbers of passengers over a wide range of distances. It would now be a much tougher proposition to sell Concorde. With airline capital being allocated to the wide-bodied jets, there would be greater difficulty in finding the millions needed to buy SSTs, and generating the huge cash flows to pay back such mammoth loans. Aviation consultant Richard Worcester knowingly predicted, "It looks as if poor little Concorde is going to be squashed between massive events!"

Boeing's other commercial project, the SST, did not enjoy the success of the Jumbo Jet. As the swing-wing mammoth of 350 seats started to fall farther behind, the Anglo-French salesmen began to feel more confident. In 1966, Burgess told a press conference that even on the most pessimistic assumptions of a total ban of supersonic overland flight, a 25% surcharge and a bare three year lead over the Americans, 250 aircraft would be sold by 1975. "But if these pessimistic assumptions do not materialise and the lead over the United States were to increase to over three years, as seems likely in view of American hesitation to start their project, there is no doubt that the sales of Concorde should rise to the 400 mark by 1980."

The airlines were only too pleased to wait for the 2707. They wanted to postpone the supersonic era for as long as possible. Concorde options stuck at seventy-four and stayed there. These options were not completely discouraging: after all they represented sixteen key airlines carrying two-thirds of the world's air traffic. Nor did they tell the whole story, because in the view of one BAC salesman—"There was no commercial advantage to be gained from taking out new options, to gain positions in an order book which was unlikely to be changed three years later. The rest of the world's airlines in 1968 sat back and said nobody else is going to come along, so nothing is lost by not taking out options. In fact they have saved some money on the interest they would have paid on the option stake."

The British Government did not like the situation and suspected that there had been too much crystal-ball gazing. In 1968 it called for a complete market break-down. There had been conflicting estimates of likely sales for too long, and the air travel business, which had been booming since 1960, was beginning to show ominous signs of change. The survey was the first depth study of Concorde's sales potential, as one of those involved indicated, "The way to estimate the market for any aeroplane, whether it was Boeing, Douglas or BAC was to look at the passenger-miles and the productivity of the aeroplane, divide one by the other, and 'Hey Presto' that was the number of planes you could sell. Our way was really no different to anybody else's." But by 1968, with the first flight of Concorde imminent, and with big decisions to be taken about production finance, nobody was going to act on a "Hey Presto" argument.

The aircraft's price was now approaching ten million pounds apiece, and it was unrealistic to establish a production line if the total market, as some experts were forecasting, might be as small as fifty planes. To bring the price down to the sort of figure the airlines could be reasonably asked to pay meant building at least 150 before overheads could fall to reasonable levels. After months of analysis with advanced computer techniques that BAC felt "put us four years ahead of the airlines", in which every potential customer's operation was studied, the benefits of buying Concorde were clearly presented. Account was taken of all kinds of variables such as inflation and worsening economic conditions. In its complexity the operation was as sophisticated as the flight test programme, measured on computer time alone, and the final reports ran to a series of thick volumes. With this detailed picture the Concorde joint committees accepted the report's encouraging predictions of a minimum market in the region of 200 to 250 planes, based on an assumption that supersonic flight would be forbidden over land. But the immediate decision on whether to buy the expensive aircraft rested with hardened airline bosses, not civil servants.

The airlines had been involved with Concorde from the start. BEA and BOAC had sat on the first Farnborough study groups and as one BOAC executive put it, "This airline has put a hell of a lot into Concorde." In 1967, the Mentzner Committee had been set up, on which sat representatives of the leading American option-holders—led by Pan American—and the influential Performance, Economics and Noise Committee expressed airline views.

Among the interesting exchanges were those about customer comforts. On the question of space for the lavatory and the galleys, the French had explained at a press conference in 1964 that by cutting out the catering arrangements more passengers could be carried. But the half-serious suggestion of "let them eat sandwiches" met with instant and hostile reactions from the airline chiefs whose competitive edge over their rivals often appears to depend on how many olives go into a martini. As one airline executive put it, "We know the airline business, and when, on that occasion, the manufacturer suggested we serve a cold buffet, it was for his own ends. We told them to go away and build their aeroplane. It was not suggested because they believed that cold meals are best, it was suggested because of making up some deficiency in the aeroplane." The planemakers, however, could not understand the necessity of trading vital payload against a five star flying restaurant, which was the incomprehensible desire of many airlines. The row went right to the top, one British Minister remembered, "Crass arguments, whether or not the airlines insisted on providing eight-course meals for everyone. The airlines finally insisted and each portion of caviar carried to Mach 2 cost pints of valuable fuel. It was this type of thing that always whittled away payload." But the airline bosses saw it differently, "Our business is to please our passengers and give them value for the money they give us. We have to attract more passengers to buy new aeroplanes, because they cost us a hell of a lot of dough. We have to get to know what the passenger wants and get that to him, and all the statements made by all the politicians won't change that fact."

The customer's needs are defined for him by the airlines, and the Concorde sales team has to face a wide assortment of managements. Some are operating national airlines for prestige reasons with little concern for profit. Indeed to be able to fly an airliner in your own bright livery seems an important status symbol for many countries, ranking second only to a seat at the U.N. Other companies, particularly the domestic American operators and international corporations, are poised on a commercial knife-edge, fighting for traffic over the North Atlantic where Concorde's technical and financial viability will be put to the test.

Concorde must show that it can carry 20,000 lb. from Paris to New York against winter headwinds on initial entry into service in 1974, with sufficient fuel reserves to stack over a crowded Kennedy Airport for thirty-five minutes, and still have enough for diversion. The first test results were all-important in establishing this simple guarantee. If they were discouraging, more than one per cent outside the forecasts, the aircraft would end up on a multi-million-

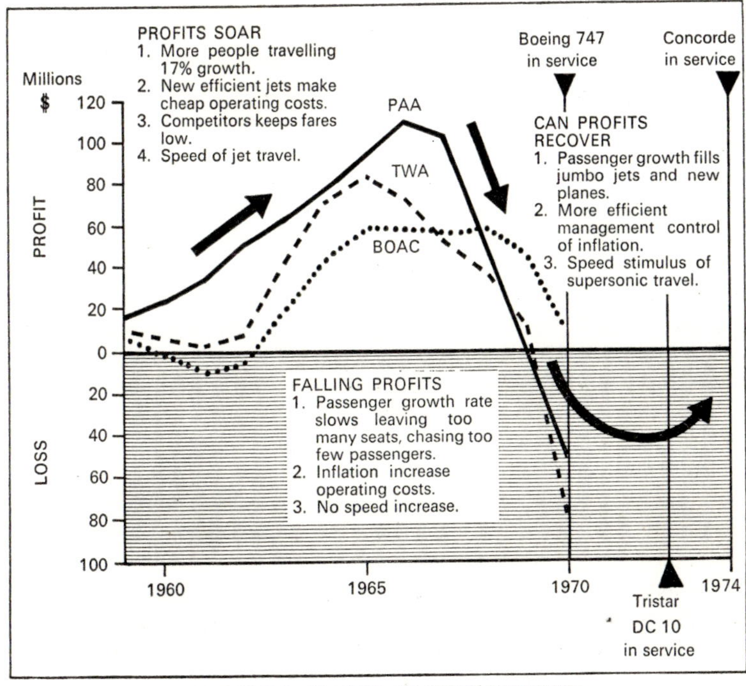

THE ROLLER COASTER OF AIRLINE PROFITS

After 10 good years, earnings dive into the red with the coming of the Jumbo Jets in 1970— could Concorde fly them out of trouble in 1974?

pound scrap-heap.

By the autumn of 1970, BAC and Aerospatiale breathed a sigh of relief when their computer told them they had pulled it off. Sir George Edwards publicly announced on television, "If anybody thinks Concorde's going to cancel itself because it doesn't work, then it isn't." He went on, "I've had a look at a good many sets of figures in my life in the same way I've looked at this lot, continuously and anxiously, and I'll stick my neck out now and say that the figures we've measured leave me in no doubt." By the Spring of 1971 enough hours had been logged for most doubts about performance to be completely dispelled. "From the point of view of chaps who want to cancel, it's rotten bad luck that the aeroplane does the job we said it would", was the observation of Geoffrey Knight, expressing the obvious satisfaction felt by his Bristol colleagues. "That would have been the really easy way out for the people who wanted to cancel."

But the airlines were not going to be satisfied that easily. Najeeb Halaby, however, was quick to point out everything that remained to be proven. "You ought to have reams of data to be damn-sure what you've got. Now let's assume that they have met the range and payload, which is a very difficult test. Then I say we have the airport noise problem left, and we have a number of minor things like the interior of the cabin. We're terribly concerned as we see the public accepting the spacious 747, that they won't want to go back to be compressed in a little tube. Finally the airline economics. Even if the payload range is met at Mach 2, when we get the speed and time, what about the profitability to BOAC and Air France and Pan Am?" In spite of all the years of research, the success of flight testing, and the massive market research of the sales department, Concorde arrived on the airplane market at a very difficult time.

BAC did not need the Chairman of Pan Am to tell them that the airlines were in trouble. The simple fact was that at the end of the 'sixties passenger traffic had stopped growing at the large and steady rate everybody had become accustomed to expect. To make matters worse, the slower growth-rate has coincided with the arrival of the "wide-bodied" jets—the 747, Tri-star and DC-10, which have increased the number of seats for sale. Airline operating profits fell from ten per cent in 1965 to five and a half per cent in 1970, with the new Jumbos flying well below their break-even load. Even a Jumbo cannot make money on empty seats; the airlines were in trouble with millions staked out on new aircraft but with cash-flows falling well below predicted levels. Few sympathised with the beleaguered managements who had grown fat and complacent in the good years of the 'sixties, when operating costs had fallen lower as new aircraft came into service. In the United States financial commentators complained of a "mañana" approach to management and started to talk gloomily about bankruptcies and spectacular Penn Centrals of the air. In 1970 Secor D. Browne, Chairman of the American Civil Aeronautics Board, said: "My conclusion is that the airlines are all right for about a year, then some of them could run out of cash. Meanwhile, we simply have to work out their problems. If we can't, there will be bankruptcies." Finding money for Concorde purchases would be an uphill struggle in a changed economic landscape. Even the options had now become vulnerable.

The salesmen are now as important as the test-pilots. Concorde is a new concept in air travel and as such demands an original approach to sales strategy. This is not easy, when the airlines are obsessed with financial problems. The aircraft's obvious selling point is its speed. After considerable computer analysis of airline records the Concorde salesmen are convinced that the supersonic airliner will help the ailing world air transport industry to break out of its depression. They believe that speed must be sold at a premium

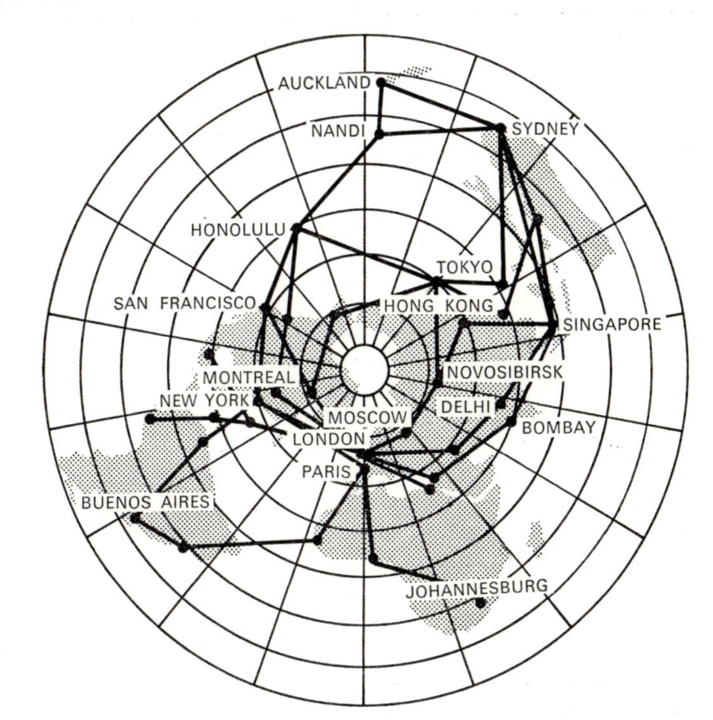

Journey-time comparison

(*including 45 minutes for transits*)

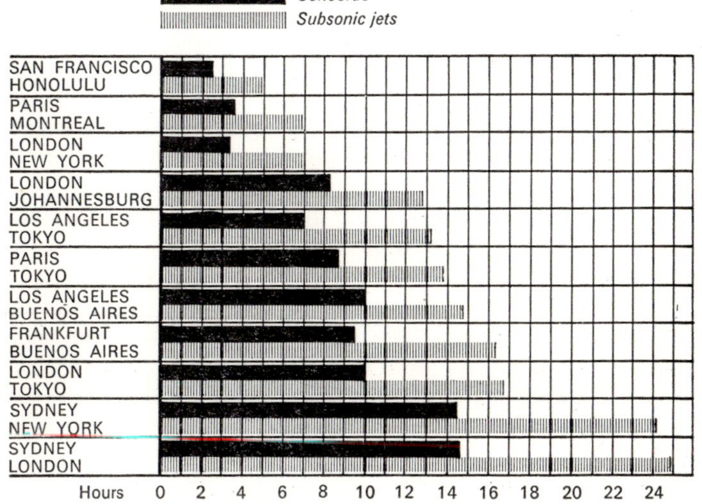

because although Concorde is one-and-a-half times more productive than a 707, crossing the Atlantic four times a day to the 707's one trip, the increased productivity has to be paid for in higher operating costs. Supersonic operation is likely to cost 50% more but this would obviously be overcome by the far higher load factors on aircraft offering a faster service.

The effect of an all-Concorde fleet would terrify the airline managers, since they would have to write off expensive subsonic jets. The solution to this problem suggested by Burgess's men is to operate the right mix of Concordes and slower 747s. The first-class passengers could be attracted to the SST, where they would receive a faster trip for their money instead of just bigger seats and free martinis, whilst the Jumbos could carry large numbers of people at present speeds and normal fares. Such an arrangement they believe would enable them to operate Concorde at a fare 10% less than the present first class tariff, while the overall efficiency of the fleet would be improved with a break-even load factor (i.e. the point at which the number of seats sold has covered operating cost) three points lower than the present rate. This can mean a profit of millions for the airlines. The modern business executive who is constantly on the move would certainly like the idea, as surveys have shown that he would be prepared to take 50% of his journeys by SST if the surcharge does not exceed 30%.

However, all of this means a revolution in the attitude of the world's airlines. One prominent member of the Concorde team believes, "They are wary of anything new, especially an SST and it's up to us to convince them that they are putting their money on a sensible bet. All we really had to prove was that the acquisition of Concorde would be more profitable to the airlines—this is still the basis of our selling. We've given them a great deal of analysis and statistical data to convince them that this is the case. What we succeeded in doing was to convince them to stay with the plane. We believe that the acquisition of Concorde will improve the current financial state they've got themselves into now." To the airlines, who are only too painfully aware of their current financial situation, the reaction is one of let's wait and see. The airlines do not disagree. "No one has completely made his mind up yet. The airlines don't have to jump into this, they will wait to see which way the 747 is going. What the airlines have to do is get the right mix—subsonic and supersonic—and there are plenty of theories about. What we will probably do is sample the business and work it out as we go along. The first supersonic fares will be changed over the first year or two until we find the right relationship. It is going to be a difficult thing to do."

Airlines are not the only ones building barriers against Concorde. Before it can enter airline service and contribute to the economies of Britain and France, it must be able to fly in and out of any airport in the world without causing air traffic control problems. This could be difficult in places where traffic jams are the rule, because Concorde could easily fritter away the time gained in its supersonic dash just waiting for the permission to land. Suggestions have been made that the aircraft should receive priority clearance because its arrival can be timed with great accuracy. This, however, is not likely to prove popular with those travellers who have to hang around in the sky while Concordes jump the queue. The airlines know that they must be assured on one matter above all before spending real money and buying the aircraft. In the view of one designer, "The biggest problem is going to be to try to lop a bit off noise levels. We've got to get the thing down to figures which are in the same ball-park as the best of today's subsonic jets, which is going to be a tough job." The aircraft's image has already been damaged by the environment lobby in Britain and the US. The sharp shooting in the New York Legislature over Concorde's side-line noise has produced doubts on whether it will be allowed to land in the United States at all. The answer of the French and British governments to this political threat promises some novel international diplomacy with the hint made in Paris that a ban on Concorde at Kennedy would mean no 747 landings at Orly. It is certainly likely to be a costly and difficult task to bring Concorde's engine noise down to the FAA limit of 108 decibels. Failure could mean that the plane could be refused permission to fly from important American airfields, although legally the plane was registered in 1963 under the old FAA regulations.

The other side of the noise problem—the sonic boom—has led to an inevitable, if sometimes reluctant, acceptance of a ban on inland supersonic flight over populated areas. This has certainly affected the American sales prospects adversely. The French, however, have been more optimistic and believe that flying over land is only a matter of people getting used to the boom. They have regularly flown 001 over Central France at Mach 2 and say that nobody in the cities even noticed. Pierre Satre, Concorde's designer, says, "We have two problems, the noise and the bang. The bang is not a real problem. The question of the bang, it is completely crazy." Noise, however, whether as engine roar, or heard at take off as the Olympus throttles are opened, or even as the boom of "distant thunder", can rapidly become a political issue, which the airlines do not wish to become involved with and the politicians are eager to avoid. One of Anthony Wedgwood Benn's acts as Minister of Technology was to issue a White Paper asking Parliament to consider a ban on supersonic flight over the United Kingdom. Before any further action could be taken on an issue which was potential dynamite, Wedgwood Benn had to move out of his steel and glass Millbank Tower, to make way for his Conservative successor, Geoffrey Rippon.

Concorde's trials and tribulations appeared to be over with the arrival of Edward Heath in Downing Street. The aircraft industry always believed, rightly or wrongly, that the Conservative Party looked upon them with more favour than Labour. They might have drawn some comfort from the views of Geoffrey Rippon, the new Minister of Technology and shortly to be appointed British negotiator on the Common Market. In 1964, when Harold Wilson's Government sought to scrap Concorde, Rippon believed that the only alternative was to end up "flogging hand-knitted union-jacks to tourists!" But the new Government, dedicated to putting Britain's economy right and leaving "lame ducks" to fend for themselves, appeared to be extremely non-committal about the whole scheme. With hints in the *Financial Times* about a Whitehall review of the project it began to feel like 1964 all over again to the veterans who remembered Mr. Wilson's review of prestige projects.

The sad collapse of Rolls-Royce hardly brightened the atmosphere. The planemakers still have a deep apprehension that the new Government is no more sympathetic to their prized aircraft than the last. In the words of one senior industry executive, "I think Mr. Heath regards the industry as a bloody nuisance that has absolutely wrecked the first few months of office for him. I'd feel the same if I was in his shoes." The collapse of Rolls-Royce did not help, but even hard-line British Government with its face turned stonily away from the supplications of troubled blue-chip companies, had to relent in the case of Rolls-Royce. The "lame duck" had to be swallowed whole by the British Government, which hardly created a happy atmosphere when the industry was seeking millions for new projects.

If the Government turned its gaze suspiciously on Concorde, its freedom of action was completely restricted by the need to treat France with the greatest delicacy and respect, because the new Conservative administration, led by former Brussels negotiator Edward Heath, was determined to enter the Common Market. It was almost full circle. Ten years had passed, Concorde was flying, and Britain was knocking on the door again. President Pompidou had thrown all his weight behind the scheme and acted in order to stop any rash move on Heath's part. In September 1970 he made a clear appeal to the British Prime Minister to declare his support for the grand enterprise and its importance for Anglo-French and European technology. The Foreign Office treated the statement with diplomatic tact,

The Opposition.

(Above) Professor Bo Lundberg: the first campaigner. *(Below)* Dr. William Shurcliffe: founder Citizens' League Against the Sonic Boom.

(Above) Mary Goldring: sharpshooter from *The Economist*. *(Below)* Senator William Proxmire enemy of the aerospace lobby.

(Above) Richard Wiggs: Anti-Concorde Project leader. *(Below)* Andrew Stein: New York's legislator against noise.

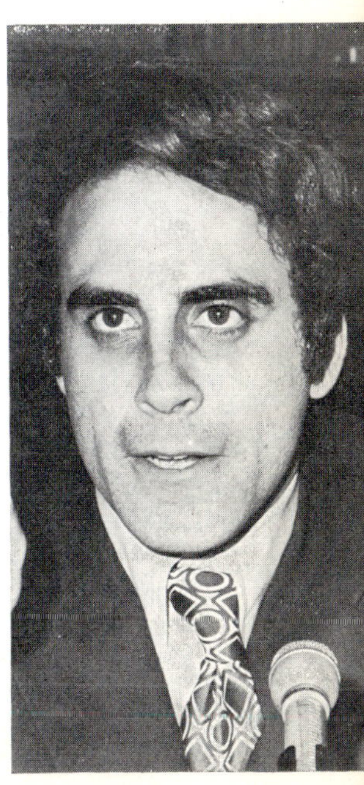

In their Sights. *(Above)* The one they killed, Boeing's 2707-300.

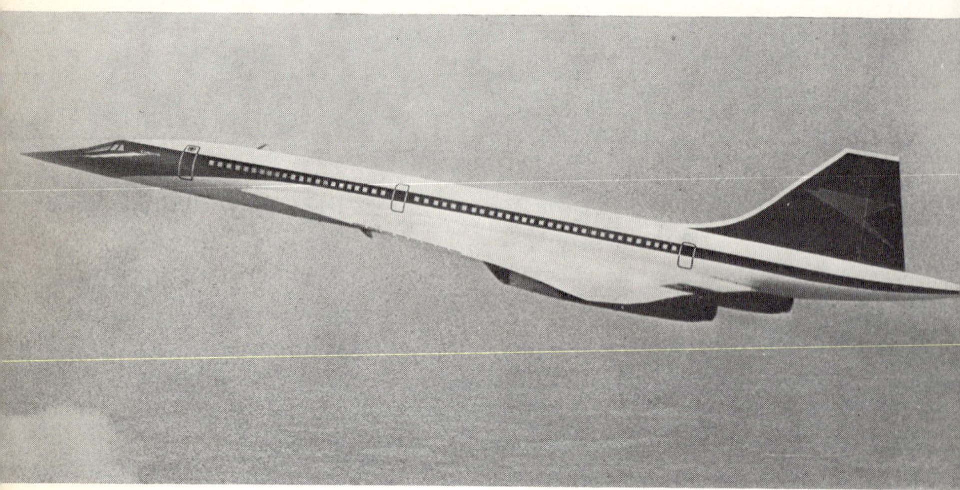

(Above) The one they tried to kill, Concorde.
(Below) The one they cannot kill, the Tupolev 144.

but the President's point was not lost on the Prime Minister. Whatever thoughts the Cabinet may have nursed secretly about the future of the aircraft, the sacred SST could not be touched while there was a chance of Britain joining the EEC. Not surprisingly, the Fleet Street rumours ceased almost as mysteriously as they had begun. The official decision was to leave everything to be decided by the flight testing and the airline managements.

The world knew that France loved the Concorde. Or did it? Signs of a growing French resistance to the supersonic idea were becoming increasingly apparent in 1970. A major attack was made on Concorde in, of all places, *Paris Match*. In a devastating editorial the magazine bluntly stated—"If it had been more closely examined its risks might have been judged out of all proportion to its benefits." In three pages of attack that might have come straight out of the *New York Times*, the magazine gave clear advice to the French Government that the wisest solution might be to give up Concorde by accepting a proposal of Senator Muskie that the United States, Britain, France and Russia should jointly agree to abandon their respective supersonic programmes. The American aircraft was still at that time officially in the race. The Elysée was furious at what seemed a clear case of treason.

Even worse was to come, with a leak in the French press of a confidential Gaullist Party report which attacked the whole rationale of Concorde. This highly damaging report was produced by Charles de Chambrun, a Gaullist Deputy who had an intimate knowledge of American industry, as well as access to highly confidential and secret Government papers. He claimed that the huge commitment to Concorde was crippling the French aircraft industry and depriving it of badly needed resources for what he saw as more attractive commercial propositions such as the European Airbus. The decade spent developing the plane would, he predicted, be looked on as a period of "missed opportunities" even of "intellectual aberrations" he told his Party colleagues. When his report was exposed by the weekly *Le Canard Enchaîné*, it shook French public opinion, which had long taken Concorde totally for granted. President Pompidou was furious, and let it be known in no uncertain terms, that blows were being struck against France's vital national interest. A counterblast in support of the project was organised, aimed particularly at the British, whom the French always believed to be on the verge of desertion.

The collapse of the American SST project worried British opinion, but merely served to encourage the French. "The SST is dead. Vive Concorde", said one French paper. General Henri Ziegler of Aerospatiale called for renewed faith in the aircraft and his trenchant attitude seemed to be justified by the wrangle which started in *The*

Times and on television, when the respected economist and diplomat, J. K. Galbraith, provoked a fresh storm by unilaterally predicting, "There isn't a chance approaching that of an icicle in hell that the Concorde will ever be allowed to touch down in American airports." It was left to the Chairman of the British Airports Authority to point out that besides a "philosophical point that an absolute zero hell might well be strewn with superb icicles, the fact is that when, and if, production versions of the Concorde are duly certified for commercial transport operations, there is every reason for assurance that the Concorde will be able to operate into and out of the United States like any other duly certified aeroplane under international agreements." *Peter Masefield, former chairman of Bristol Aircraft, went on to question whether the Professor's motives were really to undermine the significantly clear lead that Anglo-French technology had over the United States.*

The French public relations campaign for the plane had been spearheaded by the President of France himself. In April, it was announced that the President of France would express confidence in Concorde and endorse its future by becoming the first head of state to travel at Mach 2. Concorde supporters in Britain reacted with the view that it would be a national disgrace for the British Prime Minister not to do likewise. No similar announcement was forthcoming, and questions were asked in the House of Commons about the apparent lack of faith that this indicated on the part of the Prime Minister. This was denied, and the reluctance of Edward Heath to take the offer of the seat which BAC had carefully let it be known would be waiting, was explained by a curious rule of protocol—the French President had, it seemed, accepted his invitation first.

All eyes turned towards BOAC and Air France to see whether the long expected firm order for a Concorde would come. The British manufacturers had never really trusted BOAC since the VC-10 affair, when the airline had opted for 707s rather than the British aircraft, on the grounds of their operating efficiency. BAC had never accepted the British airline's case, which had meant a cut back in their VC-10 assembly line. BOAC were, however, a key airline in the Concorde campaign. If Air France bought Concorde everyone would say that the French airline had been instructed to do so by President Pompidou. If BOAC bought the aircraft it would have to do so on commercially sound grounds. The British Government insisted on this policy, and, if it was to survive against the fierce American competition on the North Atlantic route, the airline could not afford to lose money. BAC were aiming straight at BOAC as one member of the sales team believes, "First we have to sell the airplane to BOAC—and that obviously involves the

Government itself. Once that has been done, whether the Americans want it or not becomes largely irrelevant, Pan American cannot afford to sit back and take a chance that BOAC and Air France are going to take the pants off them."

But BOAC is always ready to play its cards for maximum effect. Although they are aware of their duty to buy the aircraft, if they can justify such a decision commercially, privately they are always anxious about the still-unresolved problems and do not wish to incur any penalties by being first. Their public attitude is one of cautious encouragement, BOAC's Chairman has said "We want to take the supersonic airliner if the economics and everything else in it is right." In BOAC's mind, however, there is much to be gained by foot-dragging. As the one-time Minister of Technology put it, "We had a little triangle of airlines we used to go round. Air France is bound to buy it, therefore Pan Am will have to have it and BOAC will be shamed into getting it." If the aircraft can be shown to be uneconomic to fly, and a British Government because of European interests insists on BOAC orders then the airline can feel justified in asking for a subsidy. Once before BOAC had been told to buy an aircraft—the VC-10, and the Corporation had received a large financial inducement from the Government. Such a solution would certainly please neither the Government nor BAC, because the world's airlines would claim that the plane was uneconomic. But perhaps BOAC are playing an astute game to get the best bargain, as one of its executives admitted, "After all, the Chairman and Presidents of large companies make these noises for the same reasons that politicians make them. They are only really intent on buying the aeroplane at the time it suits them, and the price that suits them. We don't want to be in the subsidy business, we want to be independent."

As the Common Market negotiations once more gained momentum in the Spring of 1971, this time with apparent French encouragement, Concorde approached a crunch decision. Work in the huge complex of plants was beginning to dry up. It was necessary to order materials and allocate resources several years ahead if even the most modest flow of Concordes was to be built. Only the two governments could sanction the release of funds for the further aircraft. Four were already planned to be flying, including 001 and 002, by the end of 1972.* After meeting his opposite number, Monsieur Chamant, Frederick Corfield, the Minister for Aerospace, decided

* By mid-1971 20 Concordes were either flying or in various stages of construction. These were the two prototypes—001 and 002, the two pre-production aircraft 01 and 02, and a further 10 production aircraft being constructed and a long-dated materials ordered for another six. There were still 74 options.

to order materials and authorise the production of four more Concordes, with materials ordered for a further six. This kept the project alive in the absence of any airline orders.

More and more, the decision is being forced back on the Governments of Britain and France. However much the joint sales team was able to convince airlines about performance guarantees, this key factor is missing—the price. The British and French governments would ultimately decide the selling price of Concorde based on the manufacturing costs, which were calculated on producing 150 planes. This would account for less than the full selling price, a profit fee to the companies is involved and a percentage to cover nearly £1,000 million spent on research and development has to be added. The civil servants would have to produce the figure. Just what this figure should be is a matter of dispute not only between the Government and the companies but between the companies themselves. The French in particular are anxious about the price of the Olympus engines, believing that Rolls-Royce may try and recoup some of its other losses on Concorde. There is obviously an upper limit to the price the airlines are prepared to pay for Concorde—and this is known to be in the region of $30 million. But even though the manufacturers can give performance guarantees, there is still no price. To the sales teams who have worked for nine years to get the customers to this point, this is frustrating. As one said, "It's wrong that it should be outside the manufacturers' control, but unfortunately it is. Every time we go to BOAC and other airlines, they come back to us and rightly say 'What is the price?' And until somebody gives it to us, the airlines can back out every time."

When the French President had left Toulouse Airport on Friday, May 7th, 1971, after a full scale send off, British officials who had flown over for the occasion with the British prototype might have been forgiven for wondering whether Edward Heath harboured a particular hostility for anything that flew. Some secretly believed that it was only the Common Market negotiations, and the newfound friendship with France that was keeping the whole project alive. As Georges Pompidou, the head of the French nation, hurtled ten miles up in the stratosphere, extolling the virtues of modern technology, "Comme simple passager, l'extraordinaire impression de securité et de puissance que j'ai ressentie au cours d'un vol qui a permis de passer au large de nos côtes à plus de 2000 Kms à l'heure au point que Brest et Bordeaux apparaissaient comme voisines", the British Prime Minister was preparing to go sailing. If he had any doubts, he was keeping them inscrutably hidden. If he wanted Britain in Europe he had little choice.

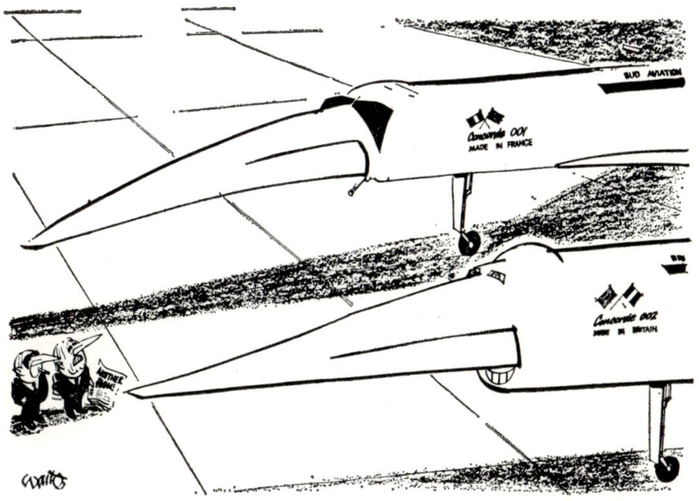

"It's the least they could do considering all the money we've put into it."

10

The Politics of Technology

"THIS IS the fringe of space where time runs backwards. We are twelve miles over the Bay of Biscay. The sky is a deeper blue than any airline passenger has seen it before—halfway to the darkness that astronauts know. It is late afternoon and we are pointing towards America." This was how the impressions of supersonic flight were brought to millions on the front pages of the world's newspapers on June 1st, 1971. In a characteristically astute move General Henri Ziegler, the President of Aerospatiale, had halted the flight test programme to take VIPs and journalists on a series of short supersonic "flips" at the Paris Air Show. His confidence paid off handsomely. The press soon forgot the Russian supersonic plane which had made its first appearance in the West a week before, and turned its full attention to Concorde. The newspapers vibrated with superlatives. Banner headlines in the *Daily Mail* proclaimed: "BOOM SHE'S A WINNER" and the normally restrained *Guardian*'s "MAN IN CONCORDE" felt excited and only slightly less awed "than the top-hatted Victorian gentlemen invited by Isambard Kingdom Brunel to sail aboard his revolutionary new iron ship."

As President Pompidou toured the sprawling assembly of airplanes from all over the world, the Tricolours fluttering over the stands and the wide variety of French-made airplanes proclaimed the growing power of the European, principally French, industry. Only in France could a major international airport be closed for two weeks to become the world's largest aviation supermarket. The centrepieces of the show were the Russian and Anglo-French SSTs. One supersonic airliner was conspicuous by its absence. Just a week before the Paris Air Show, an attempt to revive the ill-fated Boeing, on the grounds that it would cost more to wind up than to proceed, collapsed again in the Senate. Last-minute plans to put a model of the SST on show as a token of American challenge had to be scrapped. "The supersonic is a reality", blasted the *Herald Tribune*, echoing the US industry's disappointment at being left out, "The American exhibition reflecting the mood of the United States appears to have ignored this message."

Congressmen at Paris, waiting to greet the French President on his tour of inspection, recognised an embarrassing situation. They comforted themselves with the thought that the SST was "still in limbo" and that the situation would be solved because the United States could not afford to surrender its leadership in the aerospace industry. The FAA Administrator John Shaffer announced to an airline seminar: "The fact that the Soviet TU 144 is on exhibit and that the Concorde 001 has flown to Paris direct from a simulated transatlantic crossing from Toulouse to Dakar should make it abundantly clear that the age of the supersonic has arrived." This was so, "no matter how fervently certain members of the United States Congress may wish it were not so". Just before the President arrived, Representatives Henry Miller was telling reporters, "When the chips are down the United States will eventually have a plane to compete with any in the world."

The Russians were already in the field as the American politicians were only too well aware. Unofficial parties of aircraft designers from BAC and Aerospatiale tried to get close enough to the TU 144 to measure the critical areas, but the Russians had cautiously wrapped up the engine air intakes and carefully selected who could come on board for brief comradely visits. After being parked on the runway for two weeks, and following a terse press conference, it was clear that the Paris TU 144 was the only Russian prototype SST flying and unlikely to go into service over Mother Russia before Concorde in 1974. The experts were dubious about "Concordski's" payload and range. It seemed that the earlier Soviet advertisements —"The Lunokhod is not for sale—the TU 144—yes." had been premature.

Concorde may have been the centre of a brilliant publicity campaign but doubts still surrounded the project. The opposition, so long conspicuous by its absence, was growing in France. Not all French commentators felt that Concorde was assured of a glowing future. Some had suggested that it might even be a "financial Dienbienphu". The redoubtable Jean-Jacques Servan-Schreiber had published an open letter to the President in "L'Aurore" to coincide with Pompidou's flight in 001. The trip by the French head of State had more purpose than adding another page to the saga opened by Alphonso XIII of Spain's flight in one of Wilbur Wright's flying machines over sixty years before. Broadcasting to the French people at Mach 2 the President had told the French nation the plane was a success. "Today, my respect is given to you all who have given the best of yourselves to fulfil a project which honours France. Vive Concorde!"

Jean-Jacques Servan-Schreiber (JJSS), however, reminded the President that France's partners across the Channel were not so confident. Worse still, he believed that the British were not behaving like good Europeans because they were thinking of buying the Lockheed Airbus with Rolls-Royce engines in preference to the European-built A300B."How can we avoid Europe's double capitulation of England and of France, taking into account the crushing deficits of the supersonics and abandoning to America all the benefits of the Airbus market? Are we truly condemned to this aberration?" asked the Deputy from Nancy, who was not the only prominent Frenchman to think that the European Airbus was far more important than Concorde, and merited substantial investment. They believed that the Airbus was not so risky. It was well within the state of the art, being able to win a substantial return on investment far earlier than Concorde. The Europeans were deluding themselves with prestige. The French planemakers did not understand what he was complaining about, pointing to their A-300B project already being assembled at Toulouse.

If the debate about supersonic versus subsonic was surfacing in the more radical sections of the French press, it had little effect on the Elysée. The sixth French plan outlined by Finance Minister Debré contained a massive provision for both Concorde and the Airbus. "The French Government has decided to pursue the effort to its end" the President proclaimed. "How could one imagine that, for the first time in history, humanity draws back before what constitutes a spectacular and peaceful advance?"

The British planemakers, watching the stream of French aircraft take off to display their capabilities in the skies above Le Bourget, must have wondered what had happened to their own industry. The brilliant Mirage III streaked past celebrating the large export orders from all over the world. The Mercure, a brand new jet liner from the same company, Dassault, cruised overhead and few could have missed the big static display of the A-300B European Airbus. Any comfort that the British might have drawn from the occasion came with Concorde. At least they consoled themselves with the thought that they had a large share in the "great white bird", but even that was dampened by the usual French attempt to monopolise the plane, which led to a stand-up row between British journalists and Aerospatiale. The company had apparently allocated all the seats on the first Concorde press flight to French reporters. Furious at this discrimination, irate British reporters forced General Ziegler to put on a second flight for the Anglo-Saxons. At the 29th *Salon du Bourget*, Britain's aircraft industry seemed to be relegated to a poor second-place in Europe.

And yet they were not the only aerospace group to be worried. The American airline chiefs aboard 001 knew, as Turcat lifted them into the sky, that the aircraft could soon be taking off on scheduled service from runways all over the world. The British had at least one small crumb of comfort in knowing that the Anglo-French plane had achieved its major goal—to prevent the total domination of commercial aviation by the US. Although both countries started the Concorde project in 1962 with their own national motives, they had agreed about the overriding objective to resist American "colonisation of the skies". In the words of the French Minister of Transport, Monsieur Chamant, "It was the first time that two Western nations decided to produce an ambitious project which, if it goes well, as I hope, will permit France and Britain to put themselves on an equal footing with the United States in their aeronautic capacity." Britain and France felt confident that there was to be no return to the conditions of the early 1960s when they had lost the battle against the American subsonic 707s and DC-8s. The French and British were sure that when the American competition had been halted it had been as a result of technical breakthrough with planes like the Caravelle, Comet and Viscount. Concorde was planned to be in the same tradition. Now in the 1970s, if people want to reach their destinations more quickly they will have the option of doing so in a Soviet or Anglo-French jet. Europe has secured a future for itself in an advanced technological industry, and American competition is nowhere in sight. As *Time* magazine put it, for the country of Wilbur Wright, it is, "A serious break with a longstanding national compulsion

The basic reason for Concorde may be justified; it all depends on the airline customers, and with Britain and France operating two of the world's major airlines, it is pretty obvious, as

Frederick Corfield, Minister of Aerospace, believes, that "We have no intention of building aircraft to put them in museums". The British planemakers, nevertheless, wonder whether they have lost out on the Concorde project. Certainly the governments of each country entered the deal to safeguard their aerospace industries, but France seems to have created a more formidable industry, with a range of encouraging options, whilst Britain has placed almost all her money on Concorde, and the ailing Lockheed Tri-Star. France has gained much from building the supersonic airliner. In the words of Jean Chamant—"Since the end of the war we have become incontestably an aeronautic power." She now has an industry capable of competing in world markets, boosting French prestige at the same time. In many ways this has been done with Britain's help. France is now the third biggest exporter of military aircraft after the US and Russia; her aerospace sales overtook those of the United Kingdom in 1971.

In 1962 the French industry had a long way to go in learning about systems, engines, and production technique, and appreciated that the best way to learn was to embark upon an advanced project rather than working on conventional aircraft. Any visitor to the Aerospatiale plant at Toulouse will come away with the impression that France is determined to lead European aviation. The Concorde itself receives a steady stream of visitors and is surrounded by large coloured maps and charts telling how the future will be changed by the supersonic aircraft, with detailed production schedules showing four SSTs being roled out every month in 1974. In the hangar next to Concorde's, the huge A-300B Airbus is being put together and there is an immense self-confidence amongst management and staff, fostered by unwavering government support.

This, however, has much to do with a twentieth century idea of French "gloire". The French planemakers sitting over their *bouilla-baisse* and *vin ordinaire* in the canteen at Blagnac are almost personally hurt by any suggestion that the magnificent result of all their efforts will end up on the scrap heap. It would not be logical, and whatever their other characteristics the French are not illogical. Indeed there is a fierce resentment of critics like Jean-Jacques Servan-Schreiber who wants some of the Concorde resources diverted to develop the province of Lorraine. As the Gaullist paper *La Nation* put it, "Let the talkers allow the thousands of French and English to work in peace who are adding to the honour and power of their countries! "

It has, of course, been very different for the British. They have worked for years in an atmosphere of continuous criticism and doubt. The men who work on the jigs at Weybridge remember

TSR 2 and many other equally promising projects which have ended up on the scrap-heap. For Britain, Concorde has meant trying to provide a future for the aircraft industry. It is now perilously dependent on the aircraft's success. It is Europe or bust, and even inside Europe Britain may have to concede leadership to the French whose industry is in a far stronger position. Yet Britain must stay in a business which brings her over £250 million on the balance of payments every year. No one is clearer about the future than Geoffrey Knight, the chief British executive in charge of the BAC operation: "In this country, aside from Concorde, there is no Government money being invested in the civil airframe business. If Concorde is cancelled, precious little remains—a few Trident 3Bs, and wings for the European Airbus for Hawker Siddeley; and a trickle of BAC 111s till 1975 for BAC. With neither Hawker Siddeley nor BAC able either separately or together to start a civil plane on their own, the best that can be expected is the possibility that some subcontracting may come our way from Europe. Cancelling the Concorde would probably be the end of the civil aviation business in the UK."

The Conservative Government have made it abundantly clear that there is to be no more financial support for civil projects proposed by individual firms. The BAC 311 airbus was turned down, in spite of BEA and City support; and the Government has made it abundantly clear that no money is available for developing Short Take-off or Vertical Take-off planes which both Hawker Siddeley and BAC are anxious to start. With the Rolls-Royce crash and the future of the Tri-star still in doubt, the future of Europe's major engine company is far from certain. If either the Tri-Star or Concorde were to go down, it would leave Rolls-Royce (1971) with no base for future engine development. Engines cost as much as airframes to develop, and without a substantial cash flow from successful sales to the order of hundreds of millions of pounds Rolls-Royce would be unable to survive in the world market. Europe would depend on the US for its engines.

The simple fact is that the aircraft game costs a vast amount of money. Either a country has an aircraft industry in which it is prepared to invest large resources to keep its options open in the world market—or it does not. The French have adopted this approach, and have taken additional insurance policies on aircraft other than Concorde. Dangerously, Britain has all her eggs in one basket. "The French have kept their options open at very considerable cost", believes Geoffrey Knight. "Without doubt they are the top dogs now in Europe. But so long as we keep Concorde going Britain retains the capacity of taking a lead position in the next

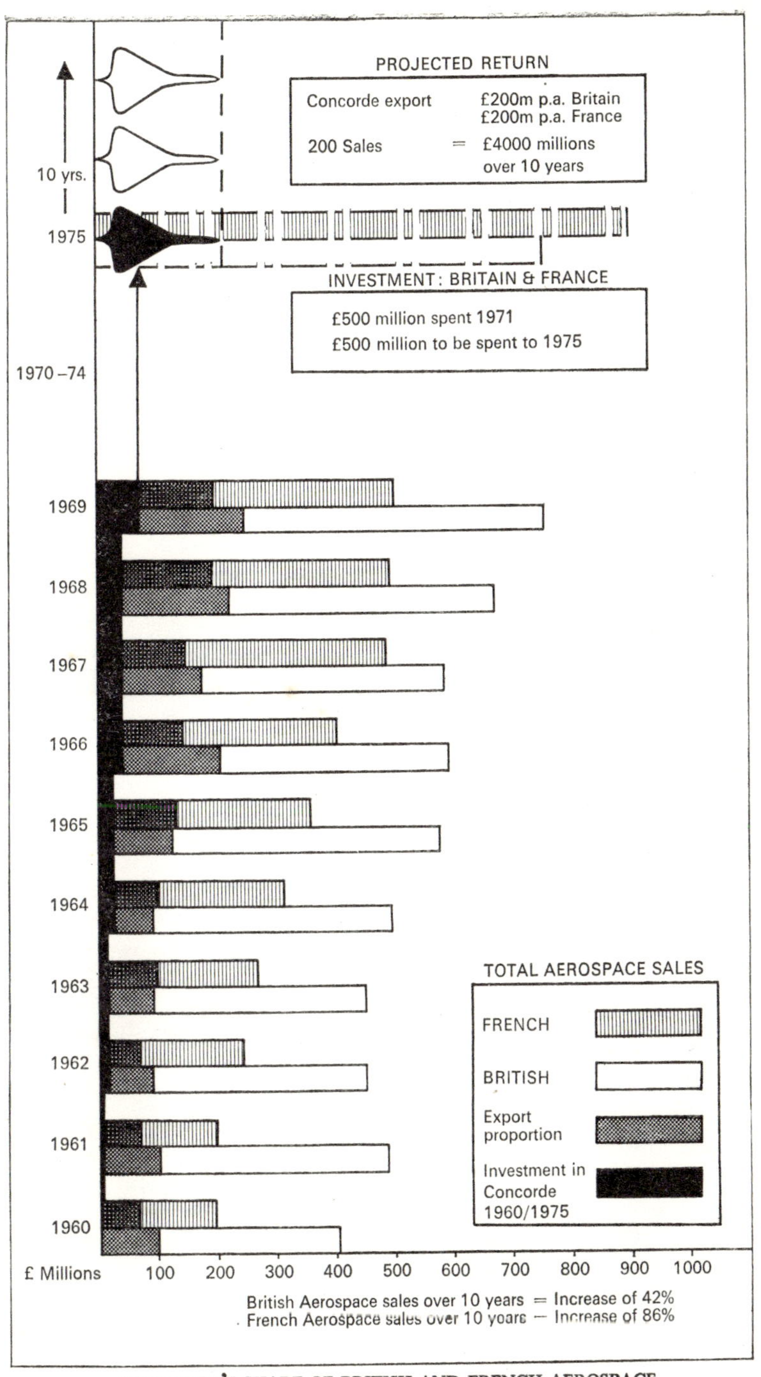

CONCORDE'S SHARE OF BRITISH AND FRENCH AEROSPACE

As French aerospace overtakes Britain's—Concorde is a big factor in both countries' export calculations.

European project that comes along; without it I don't see how we can." Britain has now got herself into a Hobson's choice situation —go ahead with Concorde or wind up the civil aircraft industry. This has come about because of the commitment to the supersonic airplane. It is argued in some quarters that one way or another Concorde will have ended up by killing the industry that it was supposed to save.

In the day and age when one Olympus engine costs as much as a Viscount, Britain needs to co-operate with Europe. Concorde started this policy, which was finally blessed by the Plowden Report of 1965. Section 523(a) called for "Whole-hearted collaboration on a comprehensive range of civil and military projects with European countries with the aim of evolving a European industry to produce aircraft fully competitive with those from the United States." If it was necessary to co-operate with somebody in 1962, France was the obvious answer, because of the parallel thinking in the two industries about the SST and American disinterest in joining any European project. The alternative was to go it alone and build more modest projects like the Dutch or Swedes, concentrating perhaps on Vertical Take-off. But there was always the belief that this could not realise the immense potential of the British industry. In the view of Duncan Sandys, Minister of Aviation when the programme was initiated—"If we're not in the big supersonic aircraft business, well it's only just a matter of time before the whole of the British aircraft industry packs up. . . . If we miss that generation we will never catch up again, we will then be making executive aircraft."

Britain has wavered between France and the United States in mounting new aviation projects, but the impetus towards Europe is unavoidable. The attempt to work closely with the American company Lockheed in Britain's other major project, the RB 211 powered Tri-Star, has revealed that there are more risks for the British industry in the political lobbying in Washington than in the bureaucratic corridors of Europe's Aviation Ministries. Britain has been kept bound to Europe by the French who would not allow her into the Common Market but who nevertheless want to work on meaningfully with Britain to build up a European industry. The foundations of this industry are now visible in the production lines at Filton and Toulouse. Britain has tried to seek other options without success.

The Labour Government were held to Concorde against their will. Coming into office with different priorities to their Conservative predecessors they decided to free the resources allocated to Concorde for other purposes. If Britain seriously believed that money and resources were better deployed elsewhere, she should have risked the Hague Court rather than accept an agreement against her will, because once the programme acquired a momentum it took on a life of its own, drawing in more and more resources. "The longer the Government were in office, the more they understood, and the more difficult they found it to find reasons to cancel", was the analysis of a senior BAC executive.

In drafting the balance sheet for the Concorde it is important to put matters into prospective. The £570 million spent by mid 1971 cannot be recovered—the value of scrap metal is negligible—even Concorde's. The money invested so far has done its work in getting the project to its present stage, providing employment for thousands and technological spin-off across a wide sector of British industry. It may be argued that the £5 per head for every man, woman and child that this represents for Britain could have been invested in other parts of the economy where returns are obviously socially beneficial such as roads or hospitals. Whilst this re-alignment of priorities must have some bearing on the future, it cannot return the £570 million* already spent. The question now is whether a similar sum for the people of Britain and France should be invested over the next few years in taking the scheme to the point where it becomes self-sustaining. If the manufacturers' calculations are right and the aircraft has a potential market of at least 250, then there is no doubt that Britain and France stand to gain a rich return of £4,000 million. But in deciding to commit these resources there is an inescapable risk—the whole project could fail for technical or commercial reasons, however much these risks have been contained.

The basic question is whether Britain should be building such aircraft at all. There are many other safer products, less advanced technologically, in which Britain could invest resources. The justification for aircraft construction lies in the enormous returns waiting for successful products; not only in direct sales but also in the "knock on" effect that a major technological enterprise brings to other sectors of industry. Normally speaking the more technologically advanced a product, the higher its return to the country or company making it. It is the labour and skill invested in the raw materials that determines the value of a finished product and aircraft are a long way in front, they are products with a high conversion ratio of skilled labour to raw material and few countries in the

* Britain's actual spending on Concorde since 1962 was announced by the Minister for Aerospace, Mr. Frederick Corfield, in the House of Commons on July 5th 1971 as £300 million. France had spent £270 million, making a grand total of £570 million. The costs are of course continually on the move and the last total estimated bill for the whole project was given as £885 million in June 1970. Inflation and other costs will inevitably change this.

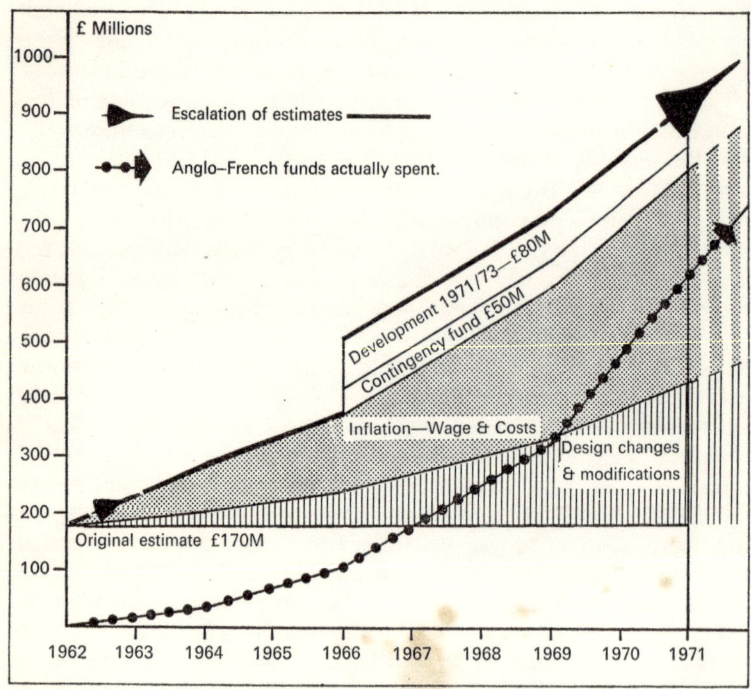

14 WHERE THE MONEY HAS GONE
Concorde estimates have soared because of inflation, design changes and development funding.

world have industries sufficiently advanced to build them. Weight for weight, aircraft are over 100 times more valuable to a country's exports than cars, but they are also much more demanding on financial resources and can be very risky. To produce a new family saloon from scratch costs less than £10 million research and development; to produce a large passenger aircraft costs over 100 times more.

This huge scale of investment may be considered worthwhile if the spin-off factor is taken into account. Because airplanes like the Concorde are on the "frontiers of technology" in a vast range of skills, they can greatly increase the whole of industry's potential. Although the American Space Programme has had no commercial objective, analysts have calculated that the huge investment can be shown to have produced returns for the US economy in new materials and techniques that have overflowed into American industry from textiles to electronics. This dynamic factor is one of the important side effects of advanced industries like aerospace within an economy. It is a benefit the French have calculated and is one important reason for the spectacular growth of their aerospace effort in the last decade. It is an effect that is not easy to measure, but having a successful piece of advanced technology in the showcase of a country's products enhances the reputation of other engineering and technological output. Concorde is no exception to this; in terms of direct spin-off it has undoubtedly put Britain and France in the front rank of industrial Powers with advanced techniques like electron beam welding, electro-chemical and numerical control machining. Electronics and avionics have been boosted by the demands of Concorde's systems; and there has been direct spin-off in areas as diverse as rubber technology and plastics. In one case, the rubber that is used to seal Concorde's windows against pressure and heat has been used to make more efficient seals for incubators.

George Gedge, Production Director at Filton, has seen the dynamic effect of the Concorde programme on British industry. "It's not necessarily the innovation alone, but how your sophisticated companies in this country in particular have been able to get into other markets because of Concorde. An example is the case of the electronic suppliers who are now in a much better position to sell to the United States." The precise impact of the development in all the fields stimulated by Concorde can probably never be measured in cash terms, but because of the higher standards of safety and reliability necessary to cope with pressures and loads demanded by the supersonic plane, all the participating firms have benefited from the higher standards. It puts them in a leading competitive position in world markets.

Important advances have not been confined to manufacturing alone, there has also been a quiet revolution in management. After the bitter triangular arguments between the Committee of Public Accounts, the Ministry and the Treasury, the PERT system of control was applied to the project with a great measure of success, with implications for better government management of expensive technology.

Concorde is, of course, above all, a political plane, as everyone who has worked on the project knows, with an unhappy tension resulting from frequent high-powered reviews, and continuous criticism from politicians and press. But whether the aircraft sells or not, if the British government intended it to be a ticket to Europe, judged by the successful negotiations of 1970-71, it has been well worth while. According to one high-level source, Concorde was on the agenda of the famous Heath-Pompidou meeting in Paris in the heady days of June 1971 when all obstacles to Anglo-French understanding were dramatically removed. Although the British have been kept in the project against their will, the amount of investment by France as well as Britain has meant that the symbolic point of no return was passed long ago, making the project a useful diplomatic card for the British Cabinet in persuading France to smile on the Common Market application. The private "Common Market" of Concorde can now become the much bigger Common Market of the EEC.

A genuine European industry has come into being whilst the see-saw of Common Market negotiations has continued over the last ten years. It is the practical result of all the intense work of the planemakers in Bristol and Toulouse. As George Gedge puts it—"It has taken a lot out of us in effort terms. The last six years all of us have worked a lot harder for a consistent length of time." The Concorde project is very much the prototype for what may be one of the first great technological mergers to occur inside the EEC. Although the administrative structure is complex and in many ways inefficient, with decision-taking diffused among the plethora of committees, and although the system is disliked by the French, as being insufficiently integrated, nevertheless Concorde's technical excellence has proven this vast rambling organisation. The system did not fall apart, and by comparison to the resources poured into the abortive American SST project even the costs look reasonable. The many barriers that have been overcome in creating the aircraft are proof of the robustness of the new European industry—language, standards, distance, logistics and above all politics have not stood in the way. This is no mean achievement, particularly when it is considered that the two countries involved have been rivals for centuries. Even if Concorde were to fail, the experience of joint working between Britain and France which Concorde pioneered will have been a valuable investment.

Other intra-European projects, such as the Jaguar and Airbus, have avoided some of Concorde's errors, but a unified management may be forced on the project by the pressure of production. The Agreement provides for this close working. Once firm airline orders come in, it is hard to see how a closer integration between Toulouse and Filton can be avoided. The day to day decisions on priorities, the exchange of staff, the standardisation of procedures together with the need to look ahead with design teams working on a stretched Concorde and a new generation of aircraft beyond, all of this will imply tighter decision-making which will be encouraged by the wider setting of the EEC. These ideas have certainly been considered at government level. In the words of Jean Chamant—"In fact, in conversations which are in no way official, the idea has been broached that Aerospatiale and BAC could eventually, if not merge, at least work together in a tighter co-operation."

If Concorde's main justification was to allow the European industry to survive, the other main purpose was to allow the European aerospace companies to work on a broader market. Decisions here depend on how far the French and British governments believe they can instruct Air France and BOAC, which possess a substantial percentage of the international travel market, to operate Concordes. In the sales team's view the opinion of BOAC will carry great weight, since it has a measure of independence in commercial operation and everyone wants to see Concorde accepted on its own performance. The position with Air France is not quite the same, with tighter French government control. The British and French industries have always had difficulty in penetrating the American market and in the opinion of one French executive perhaps the only way to defend Europe's aircraft industry is to pursue a "Buy European" policy. This is already partly the case with BOAC and Air France; in a Common Market context it could become far more significant, and may be an important consideration if there are problems with American protectionism once Concorde goes into service.

Concorde has set the Americans some difficult problems. In the case of aerospace it is becoming increasingly clear that the scale of investment needed for new products exceeds the capacity of one firm or a group of firms, even in the US. This situation was forced on the Europeans over a decade ago, but their American counterparts have only discovered it on the SST project. As each advance in technology demands a bigger and more complex stride forward, so the cost of making this stride moves from the private sector into the public. The battle of the American SST was not only about the environment but also whether Federal funding was appropriate to the capitalist ethic. This challenge was mounted by Senator Proxmire in 1963 and sustained till the project had been killed, cloaked in a quasi-environmental assault.

Participation by the Government in major future investments in the aircraft industry is going to be a difficult political problem in the United States. In Europe the precedents have been established for many years, with a mechanism for providing funds and managing the investment. In America the attempt to provide the same rationalisation wrecked itself on Republican economic philosophy. The situation of Lockheed and the Tri-star and its dependence on Federal assistance has highlighted this dilemma—the aircraft industry has become such that it needs public funding. If Americans are going to compete they will have to rationalise this need, otherwise they will become bogged down in political argument every time a major enterprise is funded by the Federal government. "Who is going to provide the aircraft for the world market at the back end of this century?" This is the question facing them, believes Geoffrey Knight. "I think that the Americans are over a barrel, because I don't think that any American company has the capability or the money to produce a new major commercial plane." Europe may now have the plane and the resources to outstrip its American competitors, hamstrung by their own philosophy. It is a situation that General de Gaulle would have relished. The tide is strongly in Europe's favour as the lead produced by Concorde is mounting to nearly a decade over any Atlantic rival. The opportunity also exists for developing second generation Concordes which are larger and more efficient than the present ones, just as the world-beating 707, which started service with a bare Atlantic range, can now fly nearly twice the number of passengers non-stop from London to Los Angeles. Concorde's builders believe she has a similarly bright prospect with a market well into the next century. As one of them said, "We probably won't know for ten years whether supersonic flight will be generally accepted as the mode of travel in the '80s. But if it is, then clearly it will be the European industry rather than the West Coast manufacturers of the United States who will be supplying the bulk of the world's airlines."

Concorde can provide work for twenty years and obviously poses a threat to American domination of civil aviation, and many Washington politicians expect U.S. SST to appear at some time in the future. They are even keen to see Concorde fly on American routes. If the sales teams turn the orders into firm commitments, and Concordes begin to operate the world's routes, there is the possibility that America will lose several billion dollars in balance of payments. However, as everyone on the Concorde project knows it must be able to overcome the local laws which may refuse landing permission in the United States if its noise level is unacceptable. This may be wrongly interpreted as protectionism in Europe. Professor Galbraith has warned the Europeans not to take the United States agreement to permit Concorde to land for granted. There might well be a backlash which is more to do with traditional American protectionism than conservation of the environment. For Britain this would be serious and crucial to the aircraft's future—in the view of Frederick Corfield, Minister of Aviation, "The authorisation or prohibition on Concorde having access to American airports is crucial for the commercial success of the aircraft." The French, however, do not regard the American decision as the make or break and believe, according to General Henri Ziegler, that the plane should fly the routes to other parts of the world. If the US does not want to be a part of this new development with all the political and economic significance of bringing faraway countries much closer to Europe, so much the worse for the US.

The Concorde has become symbolic of many things. It is remarkable for the controversy it has aroused ever since its inception. It has been the symbol of a new Anglo-French entente, of a resurgent French aircraft industry, of government competence in managing an enormous technological project and of course it has become the hated symbol of pollution for the environmentalists, who, unable to stop the motor car, can at least try and stop the next potential threat to the planet before it really goes into service.

Coupled with the commercial risk the environment factor must be taken into account, although it was hardly considered at the project's initiation. In the experienced view of Anthony Wedgwood Benn: "It was at a time when everybody in technology thought that speed was all technology gave you, faster cars, faster aircraft; but before noise and peace and quiet in the environment was what people worked for. So the aircraft arose out of an earlier sense of values." Although the sonic boom has received much attention, and potential hazards to the environment have been dramatised, engine noise can have a big effect on Concorde's immediate future. Although the plane is less noisy than some current jets, it is inevitably the target for criticism which has in turn spurred efforts to silence both the engines and the criticism. As well as rational objections, the Concorde and the concept of SSTs have stirred up the old folk fears of innovation, but with the respectable environment label pinned on. In the United States the SST is the symbol of people versus the industrial military complex, and Concorde has become mixed up in the row. However, all progress cannot be halted at the appearance of an advertisement in *The Times*, whether in London or New York. The momentum of the project is too great, and many people will resent the attempt to stop the scheme; to attack technology for its own sake is the politics of the ostrich. It is the effects of technology which have to be assessed, and in the case of Concorde the benefits could well be revolutionary.

Ever since man first attempted to leave the ground the prophets of doom have seen this as a threat to the natural balance of things. The Icarus myth is a strongly potent force in the popular imagination and it was inevitable that Concorde would find itself attacked on irrational grounds. The important thing is to distinguish genuine grounds for attack from the flights of fancy that have led to some of the wilder accusations of the environmental lobby.

The most important fact about Concorde is its survival against a background of changing politicians, airline requirements and forces of the economy. It was started for one set of reasons—as a symbol for European technology, with a limited market in the face of American competition and to the exclusion of most environmental considerations.

"Now nine years on when the aircraft exactly meets specifications, common sense tells you that now you have done it it must be pushed to success, particularly with the competition disappearing", was the view of Wedgwood Benn. "But all the elements that went into its launching have changed in the period." It is a view that BAC do not disagree with. "Whether it was by accident or design I would hate to say", observed Pat Burgess philosophically, "but the aeroplane which has come out is in fact very well matched to the late 1970's market." To Enoch Powell, a Conservative Cabinet Minister present when the decision was taken, it was politics from the start. "One hundred and fifty million pounds down, a prospect of breaking even in the long run and an olive branch to the French who might let us into the Common Market after all." In his view the project was started for the wrong reasons. "You use a truffle hound to find truffles, and a foxhound to find foxes. You use politicians if you want a political result, and business men if you want a business result." To him the likelihood that the politicians of two countries might hit upon a profitable project was about as remote as a pack of foxhounds finding truffles. But by accident or design Concorde stands at a point of significance for the future. If the market analysis is right, and in the absence of American competition and airlines having to buy speed at a reasonable price, it would not be unreasonable to expect Concorde to sell 250 planes. Pat Burgess at least is confident—"As sure as God made little green apples, if I sell one I will sell 200 planes." Selling one plane even to the reluctant Halaby of Pan Am is largely a matter for Air France and BOAC to decide.

If Concorde does sell, then there is also little doubt that Britain and France will be richer not just by £4,000 million after ten years but that the indirect effects on their economies and on that of Europe as a whole, will be great. In accounting terms. an income of £200 million a year to each country, for the investment of £25 million a year over the last decade is a healthy return. Europe could take over the leadership held for twenty-five years by the United States.

The unavoidable theme in the Concorde debate has been the management of advanced technology. It is a question which must grow in importance as industrial societies become increasingly dependent on technological advance. Progress in the fields of electronics, atomic energy and aerospace demands an increasingly heavy commitment of resources. In Europe it is no longer possible for a single nation to deploy sufficient reserves of wealth and skill to undertake a major technological advance. Concorde is the dramatic proof of this. Even in the United States, research and development have reached the point where the Administration has to involve itself in investment management; the experience of the ill-fated American SST programme and the giant Lockheed Corporation has forced the most reluctant Congressman to consider technology in a changed light.

Technology is now politics; the decision to commit a nation's resources to a particular scientific advance with the prospects of healthy economic returns is a matter of priorities and options. As Concorde has shown, decisions must be taken in the political arena to choose between possible long-term economic advantage and more immediate social benefits. This has thrust a new responsibility upon politicians and raises issues which are totally new to the electorate; the voters are now entitled to determine the fate of a project in which their money is invested. But democratic society still has to cope with the problem of dealing with the technologist, who plays the game according to his own rules. If Georges Clemenceau once said that "War is much too serious a matter to be entrusted to the generals", technology is certainly too important to be left to the technologists.

The danger, however, as seen in the fate of the American SST is the emergence of an ostrich view of technology which is an emotional rejection of all advance simply because it is based on scientific innovation. Concorde is an important test case, it offers tangible benefits and if it becomes a technological "full stop" the implications will be far reaching. No other project will appear to be safe. For the first time people will have exercised an order of priority which will be regarded as a precedent for judging other ventures. This will be, perhaps, a healthy development for democracy but if the system is faulty and the flow of information is inadequate the price could be excessive: the complex societies of western Europe with their limited natural resources depend upon the successful exploitation of their talents and skills. Technology ought to be seen as a great impetus in forcing change and sustaining economic growth, and it must be managed with care.

The logic of Concorde points to a closer integration of the productive resources of the developed world. Not only because vast enterprises demand resources greater than any one nation can now afford, but also because bigger markets are needed to absorb combined production.

In the case of advanced aircraft if a large market is not organised to satisfy the massive production investment "millions of dollars worth of aircraft could sit wastefully on a runway waiting for a buyer". When such a large proportion of a nation's efforts has been committed, it will be politically impossible to allow short-sighted airline managements to make or break the work of years. This could well be the situation of the Concorde if the British Government abdicates its political responsibility to the airlines. Long and detailed surveys either by Lord Rothschild or any other panel of experts cannot remove the Government's fundamental responsibility to deal with the issue as a matter of national politics.

It is finally a matter of international politics. Because two nations have been associated with the enterprise Concorde is still flying. If France had not kept Britain to the Agreement in 1964 the project would have been on the scrap-heap long ago. French resolve and the absence of a break-clause has kept the enterprise going against the will of British governments. This in itself is an important diminution of national sovereignty. With the British Government now turning towards Europe, Concorde will be much harder to kill.